GREAT
MILITARY
DISASTERS

GREAT MILITARY DISASTERS

CHARLES MESSENGER

SMITHMARK

Published by Smithmark Publishers
112 Madison Avenue
New York, New York 10016

Produced by
Brompton Books Corp.
15 Sherwood Place
Greenwich, CT 06830

ISBN 0-8317-4016-7

Printed in Hong Kong

10 9 8 7 6 5 4 3 2 1

Page 1: *The besieged
defenders of Dien Bien Phu,
1954.*

Pages 2-3: The Battle of
Bunker's Hill *by John
Trumbull.*

This page: *British troops
surrender in Calais, 1940.*

CONTENTS

Above right: *Iraqi troops proudly display a picture of their leader, Saddam Hussein, during the early days of the Gulf War, 1990.*

Right: *A paratrooper from the 82nd Airborne Div pauses for a drink beside his .50 cal machine gun, mounted on an HMMWV armored vehicle, 1990.*

Above: *One of the older participants in the 1990 hostilities, a M 551 Sheridan light tank rolling through the desert of Saudi Arabia.*

Military history is littered with disasters suffered in battle. Indeed, the latest has just occurred, namely that which befell the Iraqi forces in Kuwait at the hands of Coalition forces in 1990. As the 16 case studies set out in this book show, armed forces can suffer disaster for a variety of reasons. These can range from incompetence, low morale and overwhelming inferiority in numbers through to sheer brilliance on the part of the victorious commander. While military disaster has sometimes brought about the end of the war, more often than not it becomes merely one reverse among many or marks a trough out of which the vanquished ascends towards ultimate victory. As Charles de Gaulle said, when addressing his countrymen after the fall of France in summer 1940, a military disaster of epic proportions: 'France has lost a battle. But France has not lost the war.'

London, 1991   CHARLES MESSENGER

7

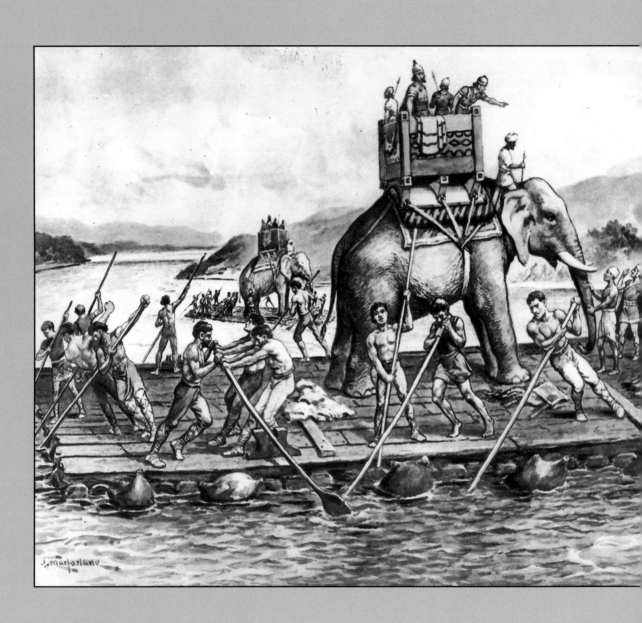

CANNAE
216 BC

The Battle of Cannae, Hannibal's decisive defeat of the Roman Army, came into prominence once more during the Gulf War when the media revealed that it was the favorite battle of General Norman Schwarzkopf, the Allied commander. Although it was fought well over 2000 years ago, it has been held up through the ages as a classic example of good generalship.

The settlement of Carthage lay on what is now the coast of Tunisia, close to modern-day Tunis. It was founded by the Phoenicians in 814 BC. They themselves came from the eastern Mediterranean, from the coastal region of what is now Lebanon and had, by the time Carthage was established, set up a comprehensive network of trading bases along the North African coast. During the next two centuries this network was vastly expanded to take in southern Spain, Malta, Sardinia, and the Balearic Islands. At the same time, the Greeks, too, had been indulging in similar schemes. Their influence extended along much of the east coast of Spain, southern France, northern Italy, Sicily and the toe of Italy. Thus, the two split the Mediterranean between them. As far as the Phoenicians were concerned, however, Carthage became the dominant city in the western Mediterranean by virtue of her strong army and fleet and commercial enterprise.

In the meantime, Rome slowly came to dom-

Previous pages: *Hannibal's elephants cross the Rhône, 218 BC. Only one survived the winter in the Alps.*

Above: *Spanish silver shekel with Hannibal's head. Spain was just one object of the Rome – Carthage rivalry.*

Below: *The course of the Second Punic War. It was waged throughout the whole of the western Mediterranean.*

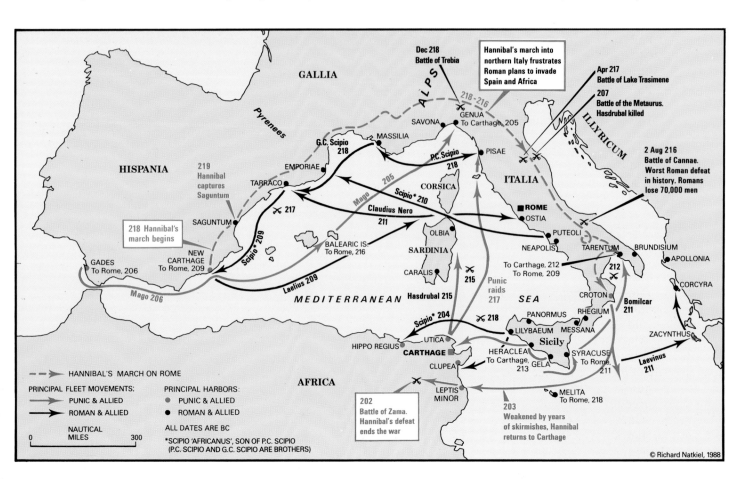

inate much of Italy, gradually overcoming the Latins, Sabines, Etruscans and Samnites, as well as repulsing Gallic invasions across the Alps. This meant that by the beginning of the third century BC the major powers in the Mediterranean were reduced to three: the Romans, Carthaginians and the Greeks. Where their interests threatened to overlap more than anywhere else was on Sicily and in the very south of Italy. Indeed, Sicily had been a battle ground between Carthage and the Greeks who had founded cities there as long ago as the sixth century. It was, however, in 281 BC that the Romans first clashed with the Greeks in the south of Italy. They enlisted the help of Pyrrhus, king of Epirus, whose object was dominance over all the Greeks in the region. Pyrrhus defeated the Romans at Heraclea the following year, largely thanks to his use of elephants, which the Romans had not encountered before, and the tactics of the Macedonian phalanx. Yet his own losses were too high. Worse, the Carthaginians, rightly fearful of his designs on Sicily, sided with Rome. Eventually, although Epirus did win further victories, including almost driving the Carthaginians from Sicily, he was eventually defeated by Rome and forced to return home.

When Pyrrhus evacuated Sicily in 275 BC he warned that the island would become a theater of war between the Romans and the Carthaginians. His prophecy was proved correct in little over ten years with the outbreak of the First Punic War in 264 BC. The cause was the occupation of Messina by a group of adventurers from Campania in Italy, who had fought in Sicily against the Carthaginians. They then began a campaign of piracy in the Strait of Messina. In order to remove this nuisance the Greek King Hiero II of Syracuse put Messina under seige. The defenders appealed to both the Carthaginians and Romans for help and the former reacted first, sending a force to Messina. The Romans, who, after some hesitation, decided that the time had come to confront the Carthaginians, also sent a force to Messina and arrested the Carthaginian commander there under the cover of a parley. Thus began the war. At first it went well for the Romans. They defeated the Carthaginians at Messina and provoked Hiero into abandoning his alliance with the Carthaginians. They overran much of the island, but could not reduce the Carthaginian fortresses of Marsala, Trapani and Palermo, since they could be kept supplied by sea and the Romans at that time lacked a fleet of any significance. They quickly rectified this and enjoyed some naval success, but not sufficient to break the back of Carthaginian seapower. The Romans therefore decided that the only answer was to send an army to Africa and destroy Car-

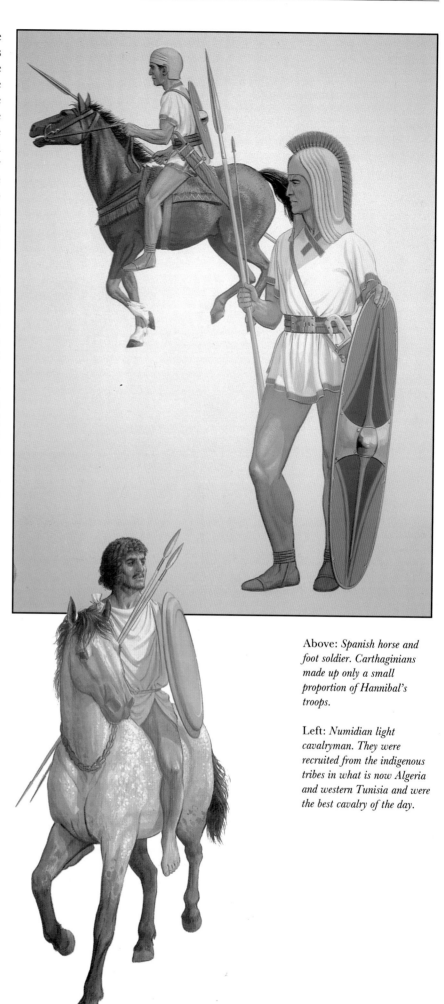

Above: *Spanish horse and foot soldier. Carthaginians made up only a small proportion of Hannibal's troops.*

Left: *Numidian light cavalryman. They were recruited from the indigenous tribes in what is now Algeria and western Tunisia and were the best cavalry of the day.*

thage itself. Consequently, in 256 BC, having defeated a Carthaginian fleet off the south coast of Sicily, 40,000 men were landed and gained a victory over the Carthaginians. They sued for peace, but the Roman terms were so severe that there was no option but to continue the war. The Carthaginians hired mercenaries and a Spartan general and defeated the Romans, who had foolishly withdrawn half of their army, near Tunis in the following year. Worse was to follow, when a fleet sent out to evacuate the remainder of the Roman forces was destroyed in a storm. This forced the Romans to adopt a more modest strategy, namely that of merely securing Sicily. After some successes, but also further reverses, a Roman fleet decisively defeated the Carthaginian ships off the western tip of Sicily in 242 BC and the war came to an end the following year. Carthage agreed to recognize Rome's right to the whole of Sicily and to keep her warships out of Italian waters. Furthermore she was to pay Rome a large sum of money over the next ten years. It seemed as though peace and

stability had been established in the region, but this was not to be.

During the last part of the First Punic War, the Carthaginian commander in Sicily, Hamilcar Barca, had risen to prominence. Having put down a large-scale mutiny caused by disaffection over Carthage's defeat, he adopted a new strategy. On the assumption that Rome would quickly attack if Carthage began to construct another fleet, he decided on a peripheral approach. Spain was to be developed to create the basis of a new Carthaginian empire. In 236 BC he and his son-in-law Hasdrubal crossed the Straits of Gibraltar and began to subjugate the southern half of the Iberian peninsula. He himself was drowned during a river crossing in 228 BC and Hasdrubal took over his mantle. He ex-

tended the Carthaginian influence northwards to the River Ebro. This began to threaten Rome's supply route for Cornish tin, a vital ingredient of bronze, which ran a little way to the north of the Pyrenees to the Greek settlement at Marseilles before being shipped to Rome. In 226 BC a Roman embassy sent to Spain agreed with Hasdrubal that the Carthaginians would not advance further north than the Ebro. Four years later Hasdrubal was murdered and the leadership passed to Hamilcar's eldest son Hannibal.

Hannibal was born in 247 BC and by the time that he succeeded Hasdrubal he had already established a reputation as a keen and resourceful soldier, well-versed in tactics, and who led from the front. He had inherited his father's long-term desire for revenge on Rome and believed that this would only be effective if the Romans were defeated on Italian soil. He therefore began to draw up plans for a march overland from Spain to Italy. He was encouraged in this by the fact that the Gauls in northern Italy were in revolt against Rome. The match that lit the tinder for the outbreak of the Second Punic War was the siege of Saguntum, a Greek port on the eastern coast of Spain and now called Murveidro. It was under Roman protection, but Hannibal ignored complaints from Rome and secured it after an eight month siege. War was now declared and Hannibal set in train his ambitious plan.

By spring 218 BC he had assembled an army of over 100,000 men in Spain and began his march from Cartagena in May. He first passed through Catalonia, but had to subdue several hostile tribes here before crossing the Pyrenees. This was costly in casualties and he also had to leave a sizeable force to secure the passes here. Furthermore, some of his troops quailed at the prospect of such a long march and he was forced to dismiss them. He was left with 50,000 infantry, 9000 cavalry and 37 elephants. Undeterred, he pressed on, forcing a crossing of the River Rhône in the face of a hostile Gallic tribe. At this point a Roman force under the Consul Publius Cornelius Scipio appeared at the mouth of the river en route to Spain to restore Rome's standing there. Both sides were surprised and, after a cavalry clash, Hannibal moved northwards while Scipio, realizing what no-one had believed before, namely that Hannibal intended to enter Italy through the Alps, sent his army on to Spain and himself returned to Rome with the intention of taking command of the forces in Cisapline Gaul and blocking Hannibal's advance south from the Alps.

Hannibal meanwhile continued to move north, along the eastern bank of the Rhône until he reached the River Drôme. Here he turned east, following the line of its southern bank and entered the Alps. His path was now barred by a local tribe, the Allobroges, and he had to fight a stiff battle in order to disperse them. Other tribes also tried to interfere with his progress and this necessitated further fighting. These

Left: *The palm tree marks this coin, found in Spain, as being Carthaginian. The horse also indicates Carthage's reliance on its cavalry.*

increase his strength to 60,000 men.

As was the usual Roman practice, two new consuls were elected for the year 217 BC. One was Caius Flaminius Nepos, who had fought well against the Gauls, but had a reputation for impetuousity, and the other Cnaeus Servilius Germinus. Flaminius's army was deployed to prevent Hannibal crossing the Apennine passes from Forli into Etruria, while his fellow Consul was positioned some 60 miles to the north-west, covering the Adriatic side of the Apennines. Hannibal left the Po Valley and, with great difficulty because of the spring floods, crossed the River Arno, he himself riding the one surviving elephant. Instead of attempting to force the passes covered by Flaminius, Hannibal marched across his front, inviting the latter to leave his sound defensive positions and attack him. This Flaminius did, but only to fall into a trap on the northern shore of Lake Trasimene and have his army destroyed. In the meantime, Servilius had been moving to join Flaminius, but suffered a similar fate. Thus, Hannibal had now brought northern Italy under his control. Rome was thrown into panic and desperate efforts were made to repair and strengthen the city's defenses since this, it was thought, was bound to be Hannibal's next objective.

battles resulted in increasing Carthaginian casualties and the nature of the terrain, aggravated by the onset of winter (it was early November when he made the crossing), caused further losses. The result was that his army was reduced to 26,000 men by the time it had passed through the mountains and descended into the Po Valley.

Here Hannibal faced Scipio, but he brushed aside his cavalry, wounding Scipio in the process, and forced the Romans to withdraw to the southern bank of the Po. Hannibal followed up and gained a decisive victory over the Romans on the River Trebia. They now withdrew south into winter quarters while the local Gauls flocked to Hannibal's standard, enabling him to

Lower left: *Another likeness of Hannibal. He fought the Romans for 17 years before his final defeat at Zama. Even so, he evaded capture and eventually died by his own hand in 182 BC rather than fall into Roman hands.*

Hannibal, however, had other ideas. His army was now only 40,000 strong and he lacked a siege train, so to attack Rome would be foolhardy. Much better would be to break up the Roman confederation. Accordingly, he advanced down the fertile lowlands on the east of the Apennines, taking advantage of the rich countryside to build up stocks for the winter. The Romans, who had appointed a dictator, Quintus Fabius Maximus, to guide them through the crisis, had now raised a fresh army. Fabius took this north in order to discourage Latin tribes from supporting Hannibal, but, unlike his predecessors, was not prepared to rush headlong into battle with Hannibal. Instead he

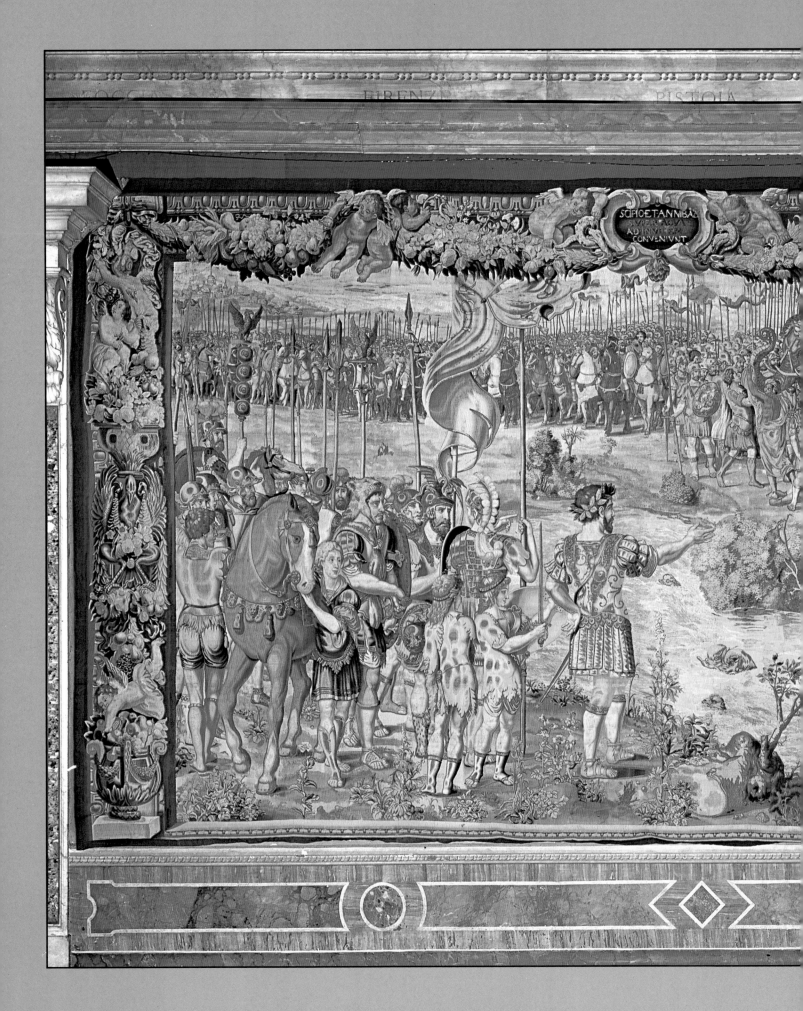

Opposite: *Scipio (left) and Hannibal before the latter's final clash with the Romans at Zama. At this battle the elephants were partially panicked by the Roman horns and trumpets, causing as many Carthaginian casualties as Roman.*

Above: *Roman legionary at the time of the Second Punic War. The secret of his success was largely his corporate discipline, but many who fought at Cannae were still raw recruits.*

Right: *A chief of the Insubres tribe. A number of tribes from Gaul joined Hannibal in order to drive the Romans from their territory.*

adopted harassing tactics, merely shadowing the Carthaginians as they moved down into Campania. Fabius, still refusing to give battle and earning himself the nickname 'Cunctator' (delayer), now set a trap for Hannibal, but he was too clever. Besting Fabius in two skirmishes, he made good his escape and continued his ravaging of the countryside. Fabius, now very unpopular with his fellow Romans, returned home, but his deputy fared no better, and, having inflicted a final bloody nose on the Romans, Hannibal settled into winter quarters at Gerunium, 130 miles south-east of Rome.

Above: *Another Carthaginian elephant commemorated on a coin. They tended to have a greater effect on cavalry since they panicked the horses.*

For the year 216 BC the Romans reverted to their normal custom of electing consuls to command their armies. The two chosen were in direct and unfortunate contrast to one another. Caius Terentius Varro was a coarse and aggressive butcher's son, while Lucius Aemilius Paullus was an urbane patrician, and a friend of Fabius Cunctator. The Senate called for a massive expansion of the army, but the consuls were to command it on alternate days, which made the drawing up of a coherent strategy, given their very different characters, an impossibility.

By the time spring arrived Hannibal had run short of supplies and so left his camp at Gerunium and moved southwards. A march of 80 miles brought him to Cannae, a town with a sizeable Roman magazine. This he took, but the Romans had followed him up and got the better of a small skirmish with the Carthaginians. Varro immediately wanted to bring Hannibal to battle, but the more cautious Aemilius Paulus, whose turn it was to command, halted the pursuit since he feared a trap. This did little for relations between the two. Hannibal now tried another ploy. He left his camp unguarded with all the baggage still in it and took his troops up into the hills beyond. He hoped that the Romans would believe that he made a precipitous withdrawal. Varro was happy to take this bait and was only dissuaded from doing so by a bad omen. The Sacred Chickens, which accompanied the army in their golden cage, refused to eat. The Romans thus set up a fortified camp, their normal nightly practice, on either bank of the River Aufidus (now Ofante), with Cannae itself to their rear.

Hannibal, realising that the Romans were not going to follow him, decided to close with them in order to force them to battle.

On the following day, 2 August, it was Varro's turn to command. Determined to have a fight, he ordered the army to concentrate on the north bank of the river, just by a bend in it, and to deploy facing it. Hannibal followed and took up position facing the Romans, his back to the river. A battle was now inevitable.

Varro had placed his infantry in the center and the Roman cavalry on the right, while the left wing consisted of allied cavalry. Hannibal's deployment was similar, but there were some subtle differences. Even though the Romans outnumbered him by two to one his 8000 Spanish and Gaulish cavalry easily outnumbered the 2400 Roman knights opposite them. In the center, as opposed to the linear formation of the eight Roman legions, he placed his Gaulish and Spanish infantry in a wedge-shaped formation, with his veteran African infantry on the wings. Finally, on the right were his crack Numidian heavy cavalry under Maharbal. His plan was to use his cavalry superiority on the left to envelop the Roman right wing. At the same time he wanted to tempt the Roman infantry into attacking in the center so as to draw them into a trap in which he could engage them on three sides.

It was a tradition that before battle was joined the opposing commanders would address their troops in order to stiffen their resolve. No record survives of what Varro said, but according to Plutarch, Hannibal appealed to his men's sense of humor. One of his subordinate commanders, Gisgo, expressed concern over the enemy's superiority in numbers. Hannibal is supposed to have turned to him and remarked that there was one thing that the Romans did not have in their ranks, a man named Gisgo. The resultant roars of laughter between the two spread to the troops, giving them the tonic that they needed.

The Spanish and Gaulish cavalry charged the Roman horse, who, hemmed in between the river and the infantry, had no room to maneuver, and was soon put to flight. Simultaneously the Numidian cavalry engaged their opposite numbers, who were forced to retreat when the Spanish and Gaulish cavalry swung round the back of the Roman line and threatened their rear. As Hannibal hoped, the Roman legions in the center began to attack. In a carefully controlled maneuver he slowly withdrew his Spaniards and Gauls until they were in a U-shaped formation. By now the Romans, whom Varro had repeatedly reinforced as they advanced, found themselves hemmed in and so tightly packed together that they could not properly use their weapons. The African infantry on the wings now drove into them. Finally Maharbal attacked them from behind. The result was a massacre. The Romans suffered some 60,000 men killed, three-quarters of their strength, while the Carthaginian losses were a tenth of this. Aemilius Paulus, who commanded the Roman cavalry on the day, was among the fatalities. In contrast, the pugnacious Varro fled from the field.

The immediate results of the battle were that Rome had lost her army and Hannibal was free to roam southern Italy almost at will especially since the Italian states began to come over to his side. Nevertheless, victory was not final. Rome managed to raise another army, initially using slaves and jailbirds, and returned to the tactic of harassment. Hannibal, on the other hand, had difficulty in reinforcing since the Roman presence in Spain diverted Carthaginian troops and they were sidetracked by an attempt to secure

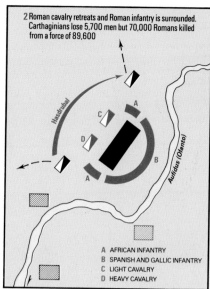

Sardinia. Consequently, the Romans gradually wore Hannibal down. With his homeland threatened from Spain, Hannibal was eventually forced to return to Africa, where Scipio Africanus defeated him at the Battle of Zama in 202 BC. It would, however, take a third Punic War before Rome finally destroyed the Carthaginian power. In 146 BC, after a three year siege, Carthage was razed to the ground and never rebuilt.

Cannae, however, marked the high tide of Carthaginian fortunes. The mighty Roman forces were defeated not only because of the brilliant and cunning tactics of Hannibal, but also partly because of the consular system. The appointment of two commanders of opposing strategies ruined any chance of a consistent long term Roman battle plan. It was a devastating victory and the double envelopment which won it is something which military commanders have attempted to emulate ever since. Hence the similarities between Hannibal's plan and the 1991 Allied ground offensive in the Gulf.

Above: *How Hannibal achieved his double envelopment at Cannae.*

Below: *At Zama it was the turn of the Romans to successfully use the double envelopment tactic.*

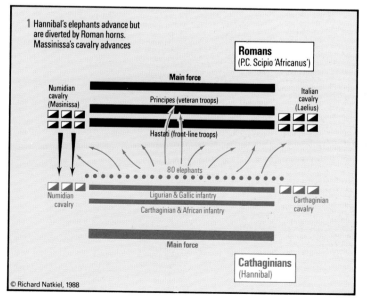

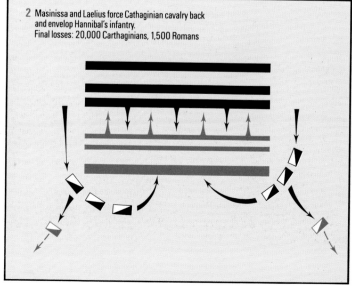

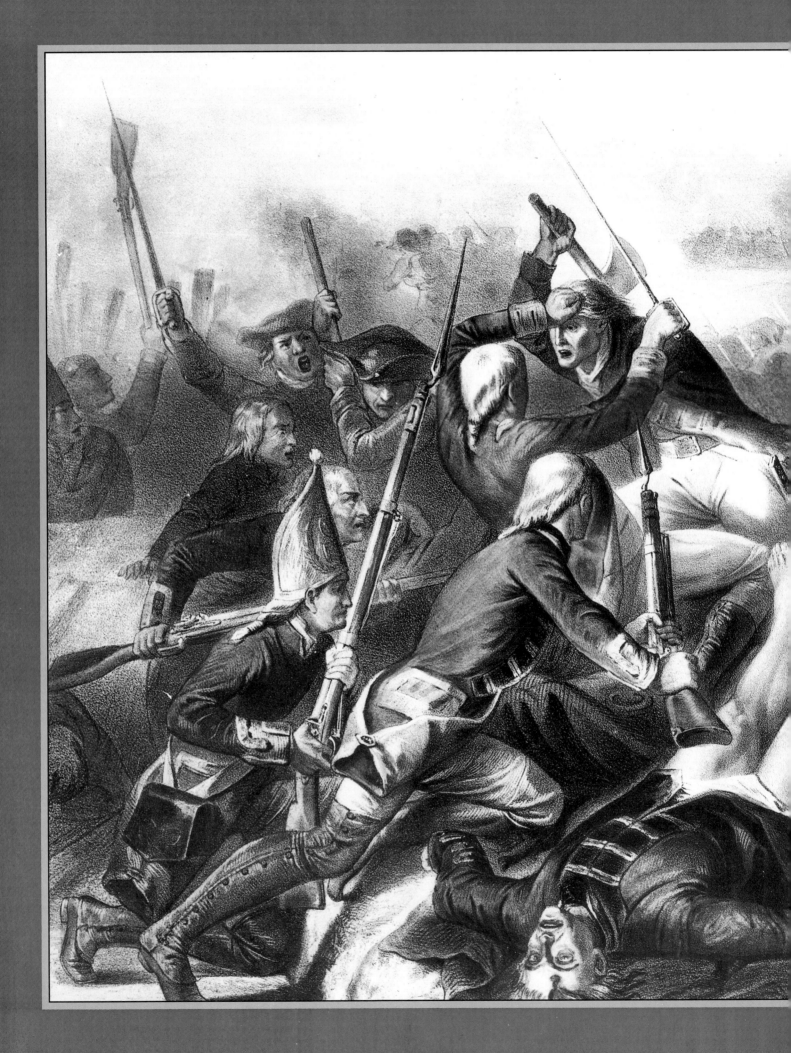

YORKTOWN
1781

MINUTEMAN
1775

Previous pages: *The capture of Yorktown, 1781.*

Above: *During the early months of the war few American militiamen had uniform.*

Right: *American regular soldier. His blue coat was selected to contrast with the red worn by the British.*

MUSKETMAN
PENNSYLVANIA STATE REGIMENT

The American War of Independence can be broken down into two distinct phases. The opening skirmish took place at Concord near Boston on 19 April 1775 when British troops, attempting to destroy a militia depot there, opened fire on American minutemen. This phase ended with General Burgoyne's surrender of Saratoga on 16 October 1777 and resulted in France declaring for the rebels.

The British, now finding themselves at war with France, declared their willingness to accede to all the American colonists' demands apart from total independence from Britain, and despatched a peace commission to Philadelphia. It was the failure of this peace mission that precipitated the second phase.

The entry of France into the war, shortly followed by both Spain and Holland declaring for the colonists in 1779 and 1780 respectively, altered the complexion of the fighting. During the first phase the campaigning was fundamentally on land, but now, with three European naval powers ranged against her, Britain faced a maritime threat, both to her lines of communication across the Atlantic and to her possessions in the Caribbean and elsewhere. Consequently the conduct of the war became vastly more complicated and this was not helped by the fact that overall command and control was still being exercised from London, 3000 miles and at least a month away from the main theater of operations.

The British strategy for the opening of the second phase was to concentrate on securing the southern American colonies – Florida, Georgia, the Carolinas and Virginia. Lord George Germain, the British Secretary of State for War, believed that the resultant isolation of the northern colonies would force them to surrender. General Sir Henry Clinton, who had been appointed Commander-in-Chief in America in February 1778, agreed with this plan, but such was the slowness of communications that it was not until the end of the year that it was put into effect.

In the meantime, Germain laid down that only the River Hudson was to be held in the north. Clinton was therefore to evacuate Philadelphia and withdraw to New York in order to block any French attempt to land troops up the Hudson. He left Philadelphia in June and George Washington, who had spent a miserable winter at Valley Forge reorganizing and training his army, immediately broke camp and set off in pursuit. He was able to catch the British, who were much encumbered with baggage, and brought them to battle at Monmouth Court House on 28 June. The American advance guard was repulsed, but, in turn, Washington and the main body saw off the British counter-

attacks. Clinton then continued his withdrawal undisturbed, arrived at the coast and took ship to New York. While he was doing this the first French contingent arrived off the River Delaware. It was opposed by an inferior British fleet, but a storm prevented battle being joined and both fleets then put into port, the British to New York and the French to Newport, in order to refit. Washington himself now positioned his army so as to prevent a British advance from New York.

The campaign in the south began well. By February 1779 Georgia had been secured and at the beginning of May the British were in front of Charleston, but the intense heat then forced a lull in active operations until summer. The French fleet under Admiral Comte d'Estaing, which had sailed from Newport to Martinique the previous November, now appeared off Savannah. His attempts to take it resulted in heavy losses, however, and in mid-October he re-embarked his troops and sailed back to France. Encouraged by this and frustrated at his inability to bring Washington to pitched battle, Clinton decided to sail south himself. On 26 December, with Lord Cornwallis as his second-in-command, he set sail with 8000 men. Bad weather delayed him and it was not until 11 February that he landed at John's Island, 30

miles south of Charleston. He laid siege to the port at the end of March and forced its capitulation on 12 May. Some 5500 Americans laid down their arms. It was a significant victory, but Clinton did not remain in Charleston for long to enjoy it. He had heard that another fleet had sailed from France and so returned to New York, leaving Cornwallis with 4000 men to continue the campaign in the south.

Unlike the previous year the summer heat did not force a halt in operations. In July Congress appointed Horatio Gates, who had taken Burgoyne's surrender at Saratoga, to command the American forces in the south. Determined to wrest the initiative from the British he advanced on their outpost at Camden, 130 miles north of Charleston. The commander here asked Cornwallis for help, which he gave. Moving quickly with 3000 men in the August heat which incapacitated almost a third of them, Cornwallis inflicted a severe drubbing on Gates. As a result Gates lost his command and was replaced by Nathaniel Greene. Cornwallis, on the other hand, now pressed on towards Charlotte, across in North Carolina and 75 miles north of Camden. At the beginning of October, however, he suffered a setback when one of his detachments was surrounded and destroyed at King's Mountain, 30 miles west of Charlotte. This put

Above: *The first clash of the war, at Lexington on 19 April 1775 when British troops, en route to destroy a militia armory at Concord near Boston, were confronted by armed minutemen.*

new heart into the local colonists and, now surrounded by hostile elements on all sides, Cornwallis gave up all thought of taking Charlotte and withdrew to Winnsborough, 90 miles to the south. Greene himself arrived at Charlotte at the beginning of December and initiated a guerrilla campaign against the British. On that note the year 1780 came to a close.

The new year found the Americans in a serious position. Greene in the south complained that he could do little since his men were starved of supplies, while some of Washington's regiments had mutinied. On the other hand, a fresh French fleet had arrived, together with a contingent of troops under the Comte de Rochambeau. Yet, the Royal Navy had also been reinforced to provide a seeming stalemate at sea. However, the British continued to be dogged by command and control problems. These were aggravated by the fact that the naval commander Arbuthnot was not under Clinton's control nor even under that of Lord Germain, but was answerable direct to the Admiralty. Thus naval-military cohesion was slender and not helped by mutual antipathy between Clinton and Arbuthnot. Furthermore, Clinton and Cornwallis had also grown to dislike one another. Germain helped to fuel this over the plan of campaign for 1781. Both he and Cornwallis believed that the sweep from south to north should continue, and he confirmed this in a letter to Cornwallis, which also allowed the latter to believe that his command was now independent of Clinton. Germain himself now believed that New York and Canada should be the priorities. Even so, in January Cornwallis began to advance from Winnsborough into

Above: *Lord Cornwallis, who was forced to surrender at Yorktown. He was later made Governor-General of India and then Lord Lieutenant of Ireland.*

Right: *The wounding of Gen. Benedict Arnold during the American counter-attack at Saratoga on 7 October 1777. Ten days later the British force surrendered here.*

L'Escadre françoise entrant dans la Delaware et chassant la frégate la Mermaid.

A La Mermaid prenant chasse.
B Le Cap Hinlopen.
C Embouchure de la Delaware.

N.ta Cette frégate a fait côte à quatre lieues dans le sud du Cap
Hinlopen, pour échapper aux Vaisseaux qui la chassoient, son
Équipage a été fait prisonnier par les Américains.

Above: *Comte d'Estaing's naval squadron, shadowed by a British one, in the mouth of the Delaware, July 1779, just after crossing the Atlantic.*

Left: *Another painting of the French squadron. Prevented by the Royal Navy from landing its troops, it sailed off to the West Indies where it enjoyed initial success, but then more frustration.*

North Carolina, Clinton having sent Benedict Arnold (who had changed sides in September 1780), with 1600 men to the River Chesapeake in order to support him.

Nathaniel Greene's adoption of guerrilla tactics had persuaded Cornwallis to split up his force and he paid the penalty. A force under Banastre Tarleton, the dashing but, in American eyes, infamous cavalry leader, was bloodily repulsed by Daniel Morgan at Cowpens, near the scene of the British defeat at King's Mountain. Morgan fell back, however, and Cornwallis followed him into North Carolina. Greene, having realized that Cornwallis was on the move, now concentrated what forces he could and set off in pursuit. In early March he made contact and on the 15th, after a series of maneuvers, the two sides clashed at Guilford, 70 miles northeast of Charlotte. Because of the dispersion of his forces, Cornwallis could only muster some 2000 men against 4400 entrenched Americans. The superiority of the British

Regulars was such as to induce panic among the militiamen and they eventually fled. The cost to the British was high, however, with a quarter of their strength killed and wounded. This influenced Cornwallis to abandon his plans of advancing through the interior of North Carolina into Virginia and he now turned south to the port of Wilmington. It was an exhausting march and many of his men were barefoot when they arrived at the port three weeks later.

Cornwallis's view, which he expressed in writing to Clinton now, was that the British had two options. If they remained on the offensive they should concentrate all available forces for a drive into Virginia, which he saw as the key. In this event there was little point in keeping substantial forces to hold New York, which should be abandoned. If Clinton wanted to go on to the defensive then the Carolinas should be abandoned and we should 'stick to our salt pork and New York, sending now and then a detachment to steal tobacco etc'. As it was, he was irritated that Clinton had not yet informed him of his intentions for the summer. While the Commander-in-Chief was digesting this Clinton decided to act unilaterally. Nathaniel Greene was still active in the Carolinas and threatening the British garrison at Camden. Cornwallis therefore decided to draw Greene away by advancing north into Virginia and linking up with Arnold.

Cornwallis set out from Wilmington on 25 April with just over 1400 men. On the same day the British commander at Camden, Lord Rawdon, also moved, his object being to prevent Greene linking up with a force of partisans under Francis Marion. He attacked Greene at Hobkirk's Hill, two miles north of the town. The British were victorious, but once more casualties were heavy, so much so that Rawdon decided that he must surrender isolated Camden and withdraw to the coast. As he did so the British forts in South Carolina fell or were evacuated and the remaining forces evacuated by sea.

Meanwhile, Cornwallis advanced and linked up with Arnold at Petersburg. Clinton's orders to the latter had been to establish a naval base at Portsmouth in order to support future land operations. The combined British force was now 7000 men, enough for Cornwallis to launch an offensive into Virginia. Yet he hesitated to do so until he had received Clinton's approval. This he requested, telling Clinton that in the meantime he intended to dislodge the youthful but famous French volunteer the Marquis de Lafayette, who had been covering Arnold with a small force based on Richmond. This he did before returning to Williamsburg to receive Clinton's reply. This arrived towards the end of June, but was not what Cornwallis expected.

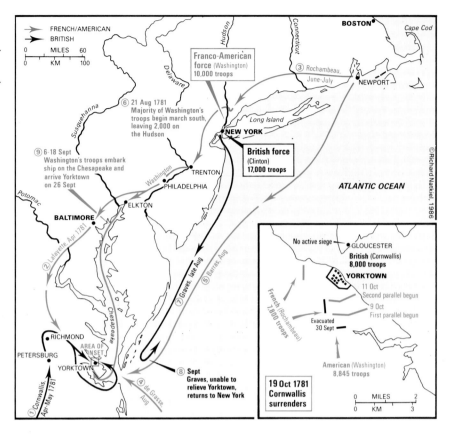

Top: *The course of the Yorktown campaign. It was eventually the failure of the Royal Navy to drive the French fleet away from the mouth of the Chesapeake, and thus evacuate Cornwallis and his men, that forced the surrender.*

Above left: *The Marquis de Lafayette. Volunteering to fight for the American cause, he was Washington's closest companion during the terrible winter at Valley Forge, and became the symbol of the Franco-American alliance.*

Above right: *Jean Baptiste Comte de Rochambeau, who brought 6000 much welcomed French reinforcements to America in summer 1780 and with whom Washington planned the Yorktown campaign.*

Opposite: *A contemporary detailed map of Washington's siege of Yorktown.*

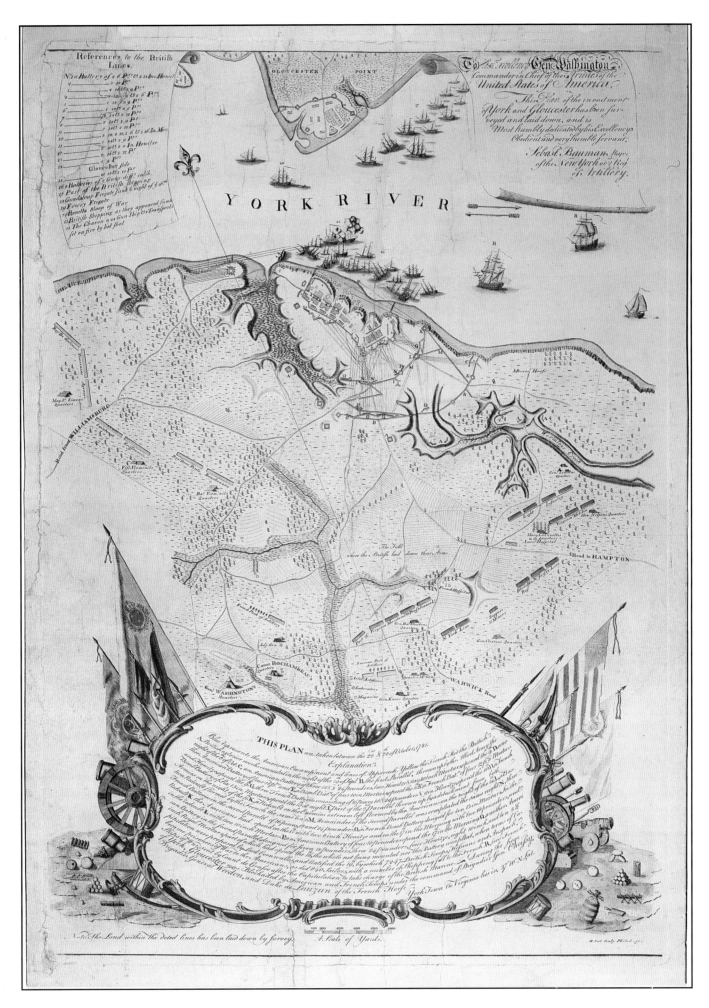

Above: *Comte de Rochambeau and George Washington (center left and right) directing operations in front of Yorktown.*

Above: *George Washington in typical 18th century artist's martial pose. His reward for final victory would ultimately be Presidency of the United States of America.*

withdrew from Williamsburg down towards the sea. Lafayette followed up, but was repulsed in a skirmish on 6 July. A further stream of letters then arrived from Clinton, many of them contradictory, which merely served to increase Cornwallis's confusion over what he was required to do. Eventually it became clear that Clinton wanted Cornwallis to establish a base at Old Comfort Point which commanded the approach to the James River. Once he had decided how many men he needed to do this he was to despatch the remainder to New York. Cornwallis looked at Old Comfort Point and decided that it was useless, especially since there was no bay there in which ships could shelter. Clinton then wrote further stressing the importance of establishing a naval base in the Chesapeake Bay area. He suggested, too, that Cornwallis could establish a second fort at Yorktown, further north and in the mouth of the York River. Cornwallis, ignoring the Old Comfort Point suggestion therefore reluctantly moved north to do this, intending also to fortify Gloucester Point, which lay opposite Yorktown on the other side of the river. It was, however, a major undertaking and Cornwallis reckoned that his whole army, together with many negro slaves, would be needed to work on the fortifications, leaving him nothing for other tasks.

What, however, of the American plans? Washington's original intention, as Clinton feared, had been to drive the British out of New York. The fact that Cornwallis had given up North Carolina and the despatch of de Grasse's fleet caused him to reconsider. Also, he had received few reinforcements for his army and began to doubt whether he was strong enough, even with de Rochambeau's help, to tackle New York. This was reinforced in early August when he heard that Clinton had been reinforced by a contingent of Germans. Then he was told that de Grasse was sailing to Chesapeake Bay, and was also given the news that Cornwallis was now at Yorktown. The result was a joint letter from de Rochambeau and Washington written on 17 August to de Grasse. Their army would march to Chesapeake Bay. Three days later they set out separately with 4000 French and 2000 Americans troops, leaving 3000 men to mask Clinton's 16,000 at New York.

Attention now turned to the sea. The British fleet, now under Admirals Hood and Graves, had been waiting to intercept de Grasse before he could land the 3000 additional troops he was bringing with him. Although Hood, on his way north to join Graves, had assessed Chesapeake Bay, it had been three days before de Grasse arrived and hence he continued on to New York. There Graves told him that Barras had left Rhode Island with a convoy of transports. Thus, on 31 August they set sail for Cheasapeake Bay,

Not only was Cornwallis not to initiate offensive operations in Virginia, but he was to send a significant portion of his force to New York. Clinton believed that Washington and de Rochambeau were combining to attack the city and had also heard that a sizeable French fleet under Admiral de Grasse was on its way across the Atlantic. Cornwallis, with the remainder of his force, was merely to take up a defensive position at a place of Cornwallis's chosing, 'be it at Williamsburg or Yorktown'. Cornwallis was understandably exasperated, but nonetheless began to carry out Clinton's instructions. He

Left: The surrender at Yorktown. Cornwallis pleaded illness and another officer represented him at it.

Right: Washington opens the bombardment on Yorktown by personally firing a 24-pounder cannon. The officer in the white coat is de Rochambeau.

unaware that de Grasse had arrived there the previous day and disembarked his troops. On 5 September they engaged de Grasse, but because of confused signals made by Graves, the senior admiral, this only involved part of the British fleet and the action was indecisive. Calm weather during the next three days prevented the British from bringing de Grasse to action once more. Next day Graves learnt that Barras had arrived. He called a council of war, which decided that the French fleet was now too strong to ensure a victory and hence the British fleet sailed back to New York. It was to be, from Cornwallis's point of view, a fatal move.

He had known on 2 September of the arrival of de Grasse and on the same day Clinton wrote to warn him of Washington's march south and undertook to send him reinforcements, as well as carry out diversions. It was this and subsequent promises of relief which persuaded Cornwallis to remain where he was. For his position as it stood was precarious. It was not so

much the nature of Yorktown itself, since this enjoyed some natural advantages. Swamps to both the east and west meant that the only feasible land approach was from the south. Here the British had constructed a number of redoubts and an inner line of stockades and earth banks

Above: 18 October 1781 – Amid the roar of cannon the British request a ceasefire and surrender negotiations.

Above: *The Americans storm the British fortifications at Yorktown.*

covered by artillery. What he did not realize, however, was quite how strong the Franco-American forces opposing him were: 16,000 men, a proper siege train under Barras as against his 7500, many of whom were sick. Also, even though Clinton had promised to send a re-

lief force it would still have to defeat the French fleet first and, in any event, ships involved in the Chesapeake Bay battle needed repair before the fleet could return, and this delayed its sailing. Without the British regaining naval supremacy in the area Cornwallis was totally bottled up.

Left: *Another view of the surrender at Yorktown. It brought an end to the fighting on land in America, but elsewhere the British did regain some self-respect with Rodney's defeat of the French fleet at the Battle of the Saints in April 1782 and the successful defense of Gibraltar, which was besieged for four years.*

On 27 September Washington assembled his army in Williamsburg. Next day it advanced in three divisions, halting two miles from Yorktown. Simultaneously another force took up position opposite the fortifications on Gloucester Point, thereby blocking a possible escape route. Inexplicably Cornwallis had abandoned three of the outer redoubts in front of Yorktown, possibly because with his reduced numbers he did not feel confident of holding them. Washington deduced from this that the British were preparing to evacuate, but it was to be ten days before the positions for the siege artillery were prepared for fire to be opened. In the meantime, on 3 October Tarleton led a cavalry sortie against the French on Gloucester Point and was unhorsed in the process.

On 9 October Washington personally opened the bombardment, firing a 24-pounder cannon. The solid shot ball flew through a number of houses before striking one in which a number of British officers were dining, killing the man at the head of the table. From now on the fire continued without a halt. On the night of the 10th/11th guns were moved to within 300 yards of the inner defenses and three days later the French and Americans each captured an important redoubt. Worse, food stocks were running low, even to the extent that all the blacks in the town were expelled, many being killed in no man's land. Cornwallis was moved to write to Clinton: 'My situation now becomes very critical; we dare not show a gun to their old batteries, and I expect that their new ones will open tomorrow morning . . . The safety of the place is therefore so precarious that I cannot recommend that the fleet and army should run great risque [sic] in endeavouring to save us.' The only option was to try and force an escape route through Gloucester Point. Consequently, in a last desperate flourish he sent out 400 men in a sally to spike the guns of two American batteries. Then, on the night 16/17 October he began to pass his troops across the river. The first wave were successfully landed on Point Gloucester, but then a storm blew up, scattering the boats. In Tarleton's words: 'Thus expired the last hope of the British army.'

Next day, which happened to be the anniversary of the surrender at Saratoga, as the cannonade continued, a white flag was raised above the British defenses and a drummer boy beat a parley. The guns ceased and negotiations for a surrender opened. Washington rejected Cornwallis's request that his troops be allowed to march out with drums beating and colors flying or that they return to Europe. Next day the garrison marched out and laid down its arms, many men close to tears, some even crying. On this same day Clinton finally sailed from New York, only to be told five days later what had

happened. He thus sailed back to New York.

Lafayette, commenting on the surrender to a friend said: 'The play, sir, is over.' Five weeks later, Lord Germain, on hearing the news, exclaimed: 'O God! It is all over!' Yet it was only after much debate in parliament that the British as a whole recognized that it was and that the American colonies had to be granted their independence. The truth was, as one of de Rochambeau's aides commented, that 'while the American people might well be conquered by well-disciplined European troops, the country of America was unconquerable.'

Cornwallis TAKEN !

BOSTON, (Friday) October 26, 1781.

This Morning an Exprefs arrived from Providence to HIS EXCELLENCY the GOVERNOR, with the following IMPORTANT INTELLIGENCE, viz.—

PROVIDENCE, Oct. 25, 1781. Three o'Clock, P. M.

This Moment an Exprefs arrived at his Honor the Deputy-Governor's, from Col. Chriftopher Olney, Commandant on Rhode-Ifland, announcing the important Intelligence of the Surrender of Lord CORNWALLIS and his Army; an Account of which was Printed this Morning at Newport, and is as follows, viz.—

NEWPORT, October 25, 1781.

YESTERDAY Afternoon arrived in this Harbour Capt. Lovett, of the Schooner Adventure, from York River, in Chefapeak Bay, (which he left the 20th inftant,) and brought us the glorious News of the Surrender of Lord Cornwallis and his Army Prifoners of War to the allied Army, under the Command of our illuftrious General; and the French Fleet, under the Command of His Excellency the Count de Graffe.

A Ceffation of Arms took Place on Thurfday the 18th Inftant in Confequence of Propofals from Lord CORNWALLIS for a Capitulation.—His Lordfhip propofed a Ceffation of Twenty-four Hours, but Two only were granted by His Excellency General WASHINGTON. The Articles were compleated the fame Day, and the next Day the allied Army took Poffeffion of York Town.

By this glorious Conqueft, NINE THOUSAND of the Enemy, including Seamen, fell into our Hands, with an immenfe Quantity of Warlike Stores, a Forty-Gun Ship, a Frigate, an armed Veffel, and about One Hundred Sail of Tranfports.

Printed by B. Edes and Sons, in State Street.

Above: How the news of the surrender of Yorktown was given to the citizens of Boston, one of the earliest centers of resistance to British rule.

AUSTERLITZ
1805

Many historians consider that the year 1805 showed Napoleon Bonaparte at his most brilliant, culminating as it did in his resounding victory at Austerlitz. True, his intention had been to invade England and this had been frustrated by the creation of the Third Coalition. Formed by Austria, Russia, Sweden and Britain, its initial strategy was to take advantage of the fact that the vast bulk of Napoleon's army was facing the English Channel, with the only other significant force being 50,000 men under Massena in northern Italy. The plan was to destroy this force and then advance into France. Napoleon's highly efficient intelligence system quickly got to hear of this and it provoked him into abandoning his designs on Britain. Accord-

Previous pages: *A birds eye view of the battle of Austerlitz.*

Above: *An English cartoon depicts Napoleon playing leapfrog with Continental Europe, but John Bull refuses to submit.*

Right: *Perhaps the most famous portrait of Napoleon, by his official court painter, Jacques Louis David. The scene is the St Bernard Pass, Switzerland, prior to his defeat of the Austrians at Marengo in June 1800.*

Opposite above: *Czar Alexander I of Russia.*

Opposite below: *Napoleon and his marshals before Austerlitz, from a painting by Carle Vernet.*

ingly, on 31 August la Grande Armée broke camp and marched east.

The Allied plan was for an Austrian army of 100,000 men under the Archduke Charles to attack Massena while another 50,000 Austrians under General Mack moved into Bavaria. Here it was to be joined by 120,000 Russians. These would arrive in three contingents. The first under Kutusov consisted of 50,000 men, and the others under Buxhowden and Bennigsen would make up an eventual total of 150,000 Russians. Mack himself moved into Bavaria on 2 September and steadily trundled westwards, unaware that Napoleon was moving rapidly eastwards. On 26 September he crossed the Rhine on a wide front and ten days later was at the Danube. Almost the first Mack knew of this was when French cavalry engaged in minor skirmishes with his own horsemen, who were covering his army which was now in the Ulm area. Napoleon, however, had ordered Murat, his dashing cavalry commander to do this in order to keep Mack's attention firmly fixed to the front. In the meantime he moved the main part of his army north and then east of Ulm, thus cutting the Austrian lines of communication. Mack, finally realizing what had happened, made a series of desperate attempts to break out of the trap, but only his deputy, the Archduke Ferdinand, was successful in breaking out with a force of cavalry, of whom two-thirds failed to make it. On 17 October, now desperate, Mack parleyed with Napoleon, agreeing to surrender if Kutusov, still over 100 miles east of Ulm, did not relieve him. Three days later, his nerve collapsed. Napoleon accepted his surrender, content in the knowledge that he had destroyed one Coalition army without ever having to bring it to battle.

Worse was to follow for the Coalition. Archduke Charles's attempt to destroy Massena failed and he was forced to retreat. Napoleon, however, sent the corps of Ney and Marmont to prevent him entering Austria from the Alps and he had to withdraw through Hungary. Thus, he was unable to influence the remainder of the campaign. Never one to delay, Napoleon pressed on after Mack's surrender and entered the Austrian capital Vienna on 13 November. The only bright spots were that Nelson had defeated the Franco-Spanish fleet at Trafalgar on 21 October (but this brought no immediate comfort to the Austrians and Russians) and that the Emperor Frederick William of Prussia had agreed to join the Coalition. This, however, was not without a proviso. Napoleon had already made overtures to the King of Prussia, offering him Hanover if he would stay out of the war and threatening to occupy Berlin if he did not. While Frederick William was considering this, Bernadotte's corps passed through Prussian

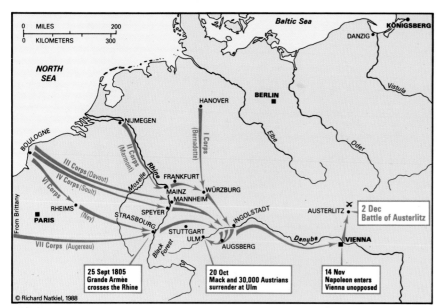

© Richard Natkiel, 1988

Above: *The arena for Napoleon's 1805 campaign against the Allies.*

Below: *Marshal Lannes, whose corps was situated in the north of the French line at Austerlitz.*

territory, thus violating Prussian neutrality. The Czar Alexander used this to persuade Frederick William to join in, but the King of Prussia would only do this if the French failed to remove themselves from Austrian territory within four weeks of the arrival of the Prussian envoy. He, however, was against his country becoming involved and delayed his departure until the day after Napoleon's entry into Vienna.

The Emperor Francis of Austria refused to be cowed by the fact that the enemy was now in his capital and so Napoleon, again not prepared to linger, left Vienna on the 15th, determined to destroy the remaining Coalition forces. All that was initially immediately opposed to him was

Above: *The phlegmatic Russian General Kutusov, who would achieve fame during the 1812 campaign in Russia.*

Field Marshal Kutusov, who had already struck once, taking advantage of Napoleon's one mistake of the campaign, when he deployed Mortier's corps on its own on the north bank of the Danube. Kutusov had attacked Mortier at Durrenstein on 11 November and forced him to withdraw across the river, albeit having inflicted heavy casualties on the Russians. Now Kutusov was withdrawing northeast in order to link up with Bennigsen, but fought a five hour delaying action against Lannes, who was pressing him hard, at Hollabrunn on the 15th. He managed, however, to disengage and continue his withdrawal, arriving at Olmutz, some 100 miles northeast of Vienna, on the 19th. Here he finally met up with Buxhowden.

On the same day Napoleon and his troops reached Brunn (now Brno), 70 miles north of Vienna and 40 miles southeast of Olmutz. Because of the need to secure his long lines of communication he only had some 50,000 troops with him. He knew that Bennigsen was on his way to join Kutusov and realized that if he did so the French would be heavily outnumbered. Hence he must bring Kutusov and Bruxhowden to battle before this happened, but in such a way as to ensure victory. He must therefore tempt the Russians into attacking him on ground of his own choosing. Even so, he would need to bring up more men, and quickly.

The view in the Allied camp was influenced by two factors. First, with the 95,000 troops that they now had they outnumbered Napoleon. Also, the supply situation in the Olmutz area was not good, which meant that the army could not stay there for more than a short time. The Czar had now taken overall command and the Emperor Francis was with him. Kutusov wanted to wait for Bennigsen, even though it would aggravate the supply problem. Alexander, however, overrode him and a plan was drawn up that was very similar to that used by the French at Ulm. The Allies would encircle the French right and cut their communications with Vienna. Thus the Allies were playing into Napoleon's hands.

The position selected by Napoleon as a bait for the Allies lay a few miles outside Brunn on the Brunn-Olmutz road. This ran through a narrow valley, to the south of which lay the Pratzen plateau, which would play a key role in the battle. Along the base of its western face ran a stream and halfway along the face was a ravine. To the south of the plateau were lakes and marshland. At this time of year they were frozen over. Napoloen deployed his army on a five mile front. In the extreme north and astride the Brunn-Olmutz road was Lannes and just to his south Murat's cavalry, with Napoleon's crack troops, the Guard in depth behind. By them lay Bernardotte's corps, newly arrived from Iglau.

The center was commanded by Soult and in the south, with his right flank resting on the frozen lakes, was Davout. He, too, had only just arrived, having been summoned from Vienna by Napoleon, with one of his divisions marching the 70 miles in just 46 hours. The Pratzen Plateau itself had been occupied by the French, but then abandoned in order to make the bait more enticing for the Allies.

The Allies, having decided to advance and seek out the French, moved down the road from Elmutz, contacted the French position and on 1 December occupied the Pratzen Plateau. That night both sides finalized their plans. The Allies, keeping to their concept of enveloping the French right flank, were to make their main attack in the south. Buxhowden, with 45,000 men, would assault Davout, while Bagration, another Russian commander, kept Lannes occupied in the north. Apart from Kutusov, who seemingly took little interest, dozing as the final plan was drawn up, the Allied commanders were confident of victory. Napoleon, on the other hand, spent the last hours of 1 December, touring his positions, his way being lighted by soldiers carrying flaming torches. Like all great commanders, he recognized the need to be seen by his troops. He had accurately forecast the Allied plan and intended to split their forces through a countermove up on to the Pratzen Plateau. All depended on the ability of Davout's men to withstand Buxhowden's onslaught.

Above left: *A French sapper (left) chats to a gunner of foot artillery.*

Above right: *A French Cuirassier. These made up the bulk of the heavy cavalry.*

Left: *The Emperor Francis II of Austria, the last Holy Roman Emperor.*

Below: *Austerlitz towards the end of the battle. In the left middle distance Russian infantry are fleeing.*

Above: *Austerlitz. Napoleon and his staff are in right foreground. Note the Austrian prisoners (in white coats) in center foreground.*

Well before dawn on 2 December the Allied forces were on the move. It was a damp, murky day and the mud underfoot hindered movement. Daylight brought with it a thick mist, which did not make the situation any easier for the attackers. Nevertheless, by 7am battle had been joined. In the north Lannes had little difficulty in holding off Bagration, but in the south Davout was under intense pressure. Many of his troops had only arrived very late the previous night and he was forced to commit them piecemeal and footsore to the battle. Yet, they held and by 10am the Russian attacks had been blunted. Now was the moment for the decisive maneuver.

Napoleon ordered Soult to get up on to the Pratzen Plateau. Thanks to the ravine running up on to it, Soult was able to get his men up to the top largely unobserved and quickly brushed aside the Russian screen on the plateau. Curiously, Soult himself was noticeable for his absence. According to one of his brigadiers, he had been very pessimistic over fighting a battle and wanted to withdraw, nearly going so far as to have a duel with his brother marshal, Lannes. Now, apparently he remained in camp, a green silk shade over his face, complaining of inflammation of the eyes. This does not, however, seem to have deterred his men. Kutusov, who, in spite of his disagreement with the strategy adopted by the Allies, was in overall command on the battlefield, saw what was happening on the Plateau and the threat it posed. He therefore ordered his reserve, the Russian Imperial

Left: *The Russians are driven off the Pratzen Plateau by French cavalry, which includes Turkish Mamelukes of the Imperial Guard.*

Right: *Napoleon (center) watches the Russians fleeing towards the frozen lakes.*

Guard, which was positioned around the village of Austerlitz, to counter-attack. For a time it looked as though this was successful, and only the skilful handling of their artillery enabled the French to hang on. Even so, Napoleon was forced to commit part of Bernardotte's corps and it was only when he deployed his Guard cavalry that the Russians were finally pushed back. Now, at last, he could go on to the offensive.

Soult's troops could see Buxhowden's men toiling below them at the southern end of the plateau. Reinforced by the Guard, they now began to engage. Davout's men also began to counter-attack. This proved too much for the Russians who, in order to escape this fire, instinctively retreated southwards, a move that quickly engendered panic. They rushed on to the frozen lakes, but the ice was not thick enough and had already been broken up to a degree by the French artillery. Many drowned and within half an hour the issue had been decided. The Allied forces began to flee to the east, with only Bagration in the north putting up any form of coherent resistance as he withdrew.

By 4pm it was all over. The Allies left 16,000 men killed and wounded on the battlefield and a further 11,000, including 20 generals, had been taken prisoner. No less than 168 cannon also fell into Napoleon's hands. The French lost 6800 men. Yet, while the Allied losses were not insupportable, especially since they still had other armies in the field, the blow to their

Below: *The map shows how the French were pressed on the wings, especially in the south, where Davout's newly arrived troops had to be committed piecemeal. The French surprise attack on the Pratzen Plateau in the center was decisive.*

morale was decisive. It was this that produced the far-reaching results that made Austerlitz such a disaster for the Third Coalition and brought about its collapse.

Emperor Francis of Austria, his country now totally overrun by the French, saw no option but to sue for peace, and asked for an armistice the day after the battle. On 26 December he signed the humiliating Peace of Pressburg. Through this he was forced to hand over Austrian Tirol to Bavaria and cede Venetia, Istria and Dalmatia to Napoleon in his capacity as King of Italy. This meant the loss of three million Austrian citizens. Francis also had to pay an indemnity to France of 40 million francs. As for Prussia, Napoleon kept Frederick William's envoy waiting in Vienna until the outcome of the battle was known. He then turned tables on the Prussians by demanding that they enter into a mili-

tary alliance with him. He would give them Hanover, but, in return they would have to hand over Cleves, Neuchâtel, and Ansbach to him. There was little that Frederick William could do, but agree. The Czar Alexander, in the meantime, took his troops home, promising to renounce his alliance with Britain. For good reason the action has another name, the Battle of the Three Emperors. Thus, the short-lived Third Coalition was dead, and Britain once more faced Napoleon on her own. Britain's prime minister, William Pitt the Younger, who had striven so hard over the past few years to forge an effective alliance against France, was shattered by the news of Austerlitz. Acknowledging Napoleon's mastery of Europe, he said: 'Roll up that map [of Europe]; it will not be wanted these ten years.' A few days later he was dead.

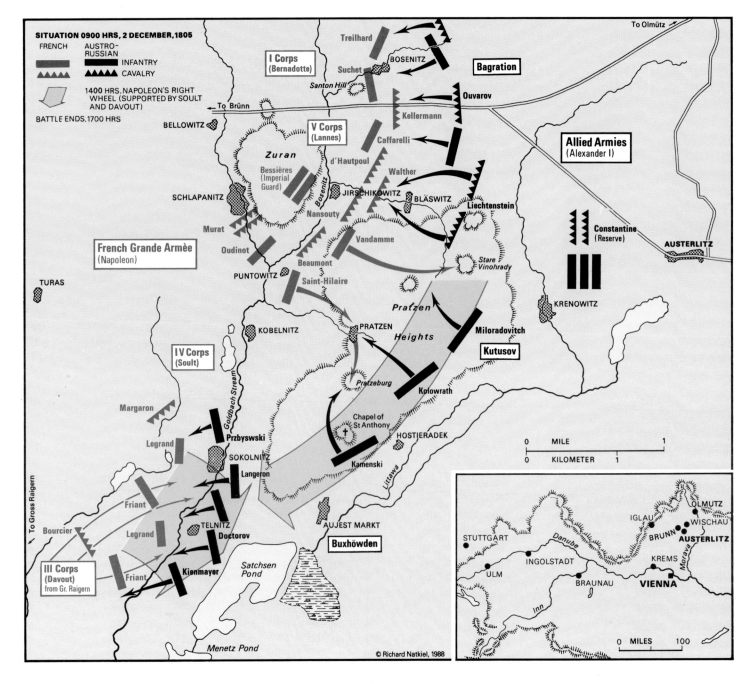

Right: *Emperor Francis of Austria is greeted by Napoleon prior to signing the Treaty of Pressburg, which marked the end of the Third Coalition.*

Below: *Napoleon and his staff. At Austerlitz he achieved one of the most decisive victories of his career.*

Napoleon always considered Austerlitz to be his most brilliant victory and, indeed, took the title of Duke of Austerlitz. No other of his battles achieved such stupendous results in relation to the cost, and none demonstrated more clearly his ability to read the minds of his adversaries. Yet, disastrous as it was for those ranged against him, it was not the end of the war. The swingeing terms he imposed on Austria and Prussia produced a canker of resentment, and while Britain still stood against him his dominance of Europe could not be total.

SHERMAN'S MARCH TO THE SEA

1864

Right: *Ulysses S Grant. Appointed to the overall command of the Union armies in March 1864, he was convinced that the only way to beat the South was to destroy its armies.*

Previous pages: *Sherman's troops enter Charleston, 21 February 1865.*

Left: *Gen Joseph E Johnston. His successful avoidance of a pitched battle with Sherman increasingly irritated many Southerners and led to his removal from command.*

Below: *Sherman's troops preparing to leave Atlanta, November 1864.*

ilitary disasters are not necessarily restricted to the outcome of one particular battle. They can also occur in other phases of war, notably in the advance and retreat. Their decisive effect on nations that suffer them can also be economic, as well as military and political.

By spring 1864 the fortunes of the Confederacy in the American Civil War, which had now been raging for three long years, were but a shadow of the bright promise of 12 months previously. In May 1863, having just won the battle of Chancellorsville, Robert E Lee stood poised to strike at the heart of the North, Pennsylvannia and the capital, Washington itself. It was the high water mark for the Confederates and the tide would soon begin to ebb. Lee duly advanced, but was met by the Army of the Potomac under General George Meade at Gettysburg at the beginning of July. Three days desperate fighting resulted, culminating in the famous repulse of Pickett's corps on Cemetery Ridge, before Lee was forced to retreat back into Virginia. Simultaneously, in a brilliant campaign in the western theater of operations, Grant had first split the Southern forces covering Vicksburg, which gave the Confederates domination of the Mississippi, defeated them, and laid siege to the fortress itself. This surrendered on 4 July, the day after Gettysburg had been won, and meant that the Confederacy was now geographically split. It was, however, by no means beaten.

In September Bragg's Confederate Army of the West gained a partial revenge for the July reverses, when he attacked Rosecrans at Chickamauga. But while the latter was forced to withdraw, Bragg's casualties had been more than his opponent's, and he did not immediately follow up his success. When he did eventually move and make contact with the Federals again, at Chattanooga in November, they had a new commander, Ulysses S Grant, the man who had taken Vicksburg, and the outcome was very different. Bragg's army was decisively defeated

and the back door to Atlanta and the rear of Lee's army in Virginia lay open. Grant's reward was a summons to Washington and a new appointment.

On 9 March 1864 President Lincoln appointed Grant his commander-in-chief with responsibility for the overall direction of the war. His mission was simple, to bring about the final defeat of the Confederates. Lincoln had selected him for the post because, unlike his predecessors and to use Lincoln's words, 'he fights'. This he now prepared to do, but in a much more ruthless manner than had hitherto been the case.

The North was still faced by two sizeable Confederate Armies. Lee's Army of Northern Virginia had some 60,000 men, as did the Army of Tennessee, the luckless Bragg having been replaced by the much more competent Joe Johnston. True, both had endured a miserable winter, desperately short of food, forage and shelter, but Grant had no reason to believe that the fight had gone out of them. Yet, and this is where he differed from his predecessors who had been too attracted by cities, these forces had to be destroyed if the South was to be finally defeated. Consequently, Grant decided to build on his successes of the previous year. While Meade, with 120,000 men, kept Lee tied down in Virginia, William Tecumseh Sherman, who had succeeded Grant in the west, would drive Johnston back to Atlanta. This would bring him into Lee's rear, enabling him to be crushed between the two armies.

The campaign opened at the beginning of May, with Grant himself personally directing the operations of Meade's army. His belief that Lee would continue to resist fiercely proved only too true. Grant's attempts to advance towards Richmond, the Confederate capital, were frustrated by the battles of the Wilderness and Spotsylvania. In both actions, which were equally bloody, Northern casualties were heavy and much greater than on the Confederate side. Lee then fell back on the fortifications covering Richmond. These proved too strong to attack frontally, and so in the middle of June Grant bypassed them and struck at St Petersburg, the key to Lee's supply lines. Here he was thwarted once more, partly because of the incompetence of some of his subordinates, but also on account of Lee's speedy reinforcement of Beauregard, who commanded here. This ended Grant's hopes of achieving anything positive himself and the Army of the Potomac settled down to a protracted period of static warfare which would last until March the following year. The initiative thus rested solely with Sherman.

Sherman's campaign took on a very different nature to that in Virginia. The more open ter-

Above: *The railroad depot at Atlanta, destroyed by the Confederates when they evacuated the city on 1 September 1864.*

Left: *General Pierre Beauregard, who frustrated the Union forces at Petersburg and barred their advance to Richmond.*

rain gave him more scope for maneuver and he was faced by an enemy whose prime concern was to preserve his fighting strength. Johnston, with his inferior numbers, was not prepared to be tempted into a pitched battle with Sherman and instead planned to conduct a delaying operation.

Sherman himself moved out of Chattanooga on 5 May, the day after Grant had commenced operations against Lee. Twenty-five miles to the southeast, at Dalton, Georgia stood Johnston in a strong defensive position screened by mountains. Sherman was too shrewd a commander to tackle him frontally and tried to hook round to the south. Johnston foresaw this and withdrew, fighting delaying actions as he went. Sherman became increasingly frustrated. Finally, towards the end of June, he came up against

Johnston in another strong position on Kenesaw Mountain, 25 miles northwest of Atlanta. Sherman lost his patience and attacked, only to be speedily rebuffed with the loss of 2000 men. It was a mistake that he was careful not to repeat.

Johnston was conducting operations with great military skill, but many Southerners did not see it that way. Steadfast in their belief that a Confederate could lick at least three Yankees, they grew frustrated by Johnston's unwillingness to fight. The grumbling grew and threatened President Jefferson Davis's position. The result was a fatal mistake. Davis replaced Johnston with the headstrong John B Hood on the grounds that he would be certain to bring Sherman to battle. Hood lived up to this expectation, attacking Sherman twice at Peach-

Below: *Another view of the destroyed railroad depot at Atlanta. It was the detonation of several cars filled with munitions which caused the damage.*

tree Creek on 20 and 22 July. Both sides claimed a victory, but it was Hood who was forced to withdraw into Atlanta itself. Sherman now swung round to cut the railways leading into it and Hood was eventually, on 1 September, forced to leave this jewel in the Southern crown to its fate in order to save his army.

The loss of Atlanta was a grievous blow for the South. But while Lee was frustrating Grant, there had been other reverses. Grant, in order to make life more difficult for Lee, had detached Sheridan with 50,000 men to finally bring under control the Shenandoah Valley, for so long Lee's playground and major source of supplies. Sheridan carried out a scorched earth policy. Initially the Confederates left him alone, but twice in the latter half of September they attacked him, at Winchester and Fisher's Hill, and were defeated. By the end of the month much of the valley had been laid waste, but on

Left: *Part of the Confederate defenses outside Atlanta after their abandonment.*

Below: *The route of Sherman's march through Georgia and his subsequent advance northwards through the Carolinas.*

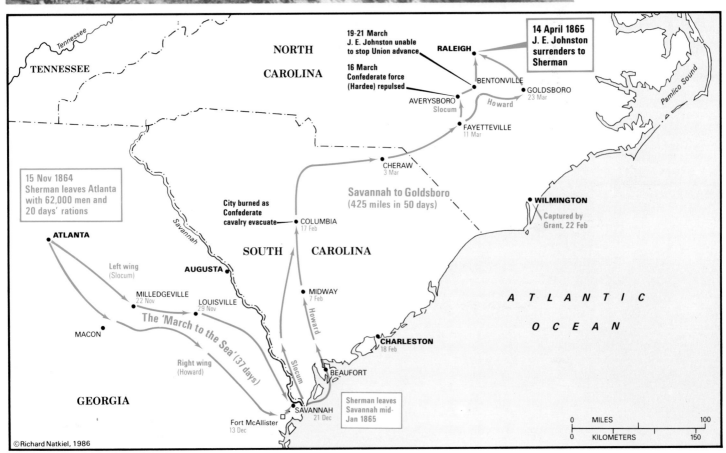

© Richard Natkiel, 1986

19 October Jubal Early, having received re-inforcements, attacked once more, at Cedar Creek. He was once more defeated and with-drew. The Shenandoah Valley was now firmly under Federal control. Also, in August, Mobile Bay, one of the last Confederate ports open to blockade runners, had been seized by the North. These successes came just in time for Lincoln, who was faced with a Presidential elec-tion in November. Indeed, because of the seem-ing stalemate during the summer, he had doubted whether he had sufficient support to be re-elected. As it was, he gained an overwhelm-ing victory over General George B McClellan.

Even so, Lee's and Hood's armies still re-mained intact and it was clear that Grant, espe-cially with winter now coming on, had little chance of quickly breaking the deadlock with Lee. Sherman, too, did not believe that he had sufficient troops to corner Hood. Indeed, Hood had now begun to march north towards Ten-nessee and Sherman's extended supply lines were under threat. There was, in Sherman's mind, one way in which he could retain the in-itiative. He proposed to Grant that he make a lightning march to the port of Savannah. He would take no supplies with him and merely live off the land, destroying what his troops did not eat. In this way supplies to Lee would be denied and he would be attacking the very spirit of the South. 'I can make the march, and make Geor-gia howl!'

Grant and Lincoln reluctantly agreed to this

Left: *William Tecumseh Sherman.*

Below: *Sherman leaves his mark on a Southern town.*

Bottom: *A Union battery undergoing gun drills under Sherman's watchful eye (in background) in an abandoned Confederate fortification outside Atlanta.*

Left: *President Abraham Lincoln and his senior commanders, 1865. Sherman is behind him to his right; Grant is on his left.*

Right: *Sherman's troops destroying a railroad. The US Civil War was the first conflict in which the railroad played a significant role, both in resupplying armies and in redeploying them. The destruction of the Southern railroads also paralysed what economic life still remained.*

plan and on 15 November, having put Atlanta to the torch, he marched out, his bands playing 'John Brown's Body'. In order to take care of Hood, he had despatched Thomas with 30,000 men to block him at Nashville. Sherman advanced on a 60 mile front and literally cut a swathe through Georgia. Each brigade provided a foraging company which operated a few miles either side of the brigade's axis of advance. At the end of each day they presented their haul of diary produce, vegetables and livestock to the commissariat. What they could not carry off, they killed or destroyed. Factories, depots, warehouses, bridges and barns were all razed to the ground, and looters made life a misery for the unfortunate Southerners who resided in the path of the advance. Railway track was pulled up, heated over fires and then wrapped round trees in what were called 'Sherman hairpins' or 'Jeff Davis neckties'.

The Georgians, who had not previously experienced the war at first hand, were made only too aware that, to use Sherman's adjective, it was 'hell'. Worse, the South had virtually no troops who could oppose Sherman, and his men, who called themselves 'Sherman's Bummmers', reveled in an carnival atmosphere.

On 10 December Sherman reached Savannah and three days later, having seized Fort McAllister to the south, made contact with Admiral John A Dahlgren's Union fleet. On the 22nd he sent a telegram to Lincoln: 'I beg to present you as a Christmas gift the city of Savannah, with 150 heavy guns and plenty of ammunition, also

about 25,000 bales of cotton.' He had dealt the South a mortal blow, both to its economy and to its morale. As if to reinforce this, on 15 and 16 December, Thomas attacked Hood outside Nashville, inflicted heavy casualties on him, and during the ensuing pursuit destroyed his army. The last chapter of the war was now about to be written.

Sherman now planned to advance north in order to pose a direct threat to Lee's rear. He hoped to be able to move in early January, but bad weather delayed him until 1 February. His

route was to take him through the Carolinas and their inhabitants were to suffer even more than Georgia had. This was especially so in South Carolina, whom Northerners saw as the main perpetrator of the war. Columbia, the state capital and scene of the signing of the Ordinance of Secession in December 1860, was literally razed to the ground. Not until Sherman got into North Carolina was there any attempt to oppose him. In an act of desperation Jefferson Davis had recalled Johnston to active duty and tried to block Sherman at Bentonville on 19 March, but the Federals proved too strong and he was forced to withdraw.

On 27 and 28 March Lincoln, Grant, Sherman and Admiral Porter conferred on board the *River Queen* at City Point near Petersburg in order to agree the conduct of the final stage. Grant now sent Sheridan to cut the two remaining railways keeping Lee supplied in the Richmond – Petersburg area. Lee sent Pickett to forestall him, but he was defeated at Five Forks, 15 miles west of Petersburg, on 1 April. Lee's last hope lay in moving out and linking up with Johnston in order to turn on Sherman. Sheridan moved too quickly for him and blocked his route at Appomattox. There, on 9 April 1865, Lee finally surrendered, as did Johnston to Sherman on the 26th. The war was over.

In retrospect it was probably Pickett's failure on the third day of Gettysburg which was the main turning point of the war. At the time, though, the South did not recognize this and continued to believe that they would eventually win, even with an ever-tightening northern blockade. The final nail in the coffin, and the one that made the Confederates finally realize that all was up, was Sherman's march to the sea. Not only did it ruin what was left of the Southern economy, but it provided a stark demonstration of total war and destroyed all hope for the Confederacy. It was therefore a disaster, especially in the South's inability to do anything to even restrict the scope of Sherman's operations.

Top: *Sherman's troops enter Columbia, capital of South Carolina on 17 February 1865. They burned it.*

Above and left: *The fall of Charleston, South Carolina, one of the few remaining Southern ports. Prolonged bombardment by the Federal Navy and Sherman's destruction of the railroads leading to it, forced its inhabitants to evacuate it and its outlying forces were occupied.*

SEDAN
1870

During the nineteenth century one means of assessing which army was considered to be the finest, was to look at the uniforms of other nations, who often emulated those of the foremost European power. In the 1860s France was that country, and several other nations adopted the French *képi*, loose-bottomed trousers, and long coat. Several American Civil War armies went even further, raising regiments of Zouaves with their distinctive baggy trousers. This trend had begun with French victories over the Austrian Army at Magenta and Solferino in 1859 during the struggle by the northern Italian states to rid themselves of Austrian domination.

The secret of the French success was seen by them to be a particular and unique abstract quality with which the French soldier was im-

Previous pages: *Prussian troops storm a street barricade to enter Paris, 1870.*

Above: *General Helmuth von Moltke, the Prussian mastermind behind France's defeat, and fellow member of the Great General Staff Vogel de Falkenstein.*

Left: *The uniforms of French Army in 1870 echoed many from Napoleon Bonaparte's era. The only significant difference was the presence of colonial troops from French North Africa.*

bued. The man who put his finger on this was an infantry officer and veteran of the Crimean War and campaigns in Africa, Ardant du Picq. He, like Napoleon Bonaparte, emphasized the moral force in war and saw it as the ability to advance under fire, arguing that it was this that brought about victory. The French soldier had this quality more so than those of other nations and it was his particular dash or *élan* which provided it.

Yet in the 1860s another army began to look like matching that of France. The driving force behind this was King Wilhelm I who came to the Prussian throne in 1861 determined to bind the German states into one under his leadership and remove the influence of Austria. His instrument for this was to be the Prussian army, which, in his words, was to be 'the Prussian nation in arms'. Within five years he had gone some way towards achieving his objective. In 1864, in a brief war against Denmark, and with the assistance of Austria, Schleswig-Holstein was wrested from her. The duchies were now shared between Austria and Prussia, but not for long. In June 1866 Prussia went to war with Austria and decisively defeated her at the Battle of Königgratz. What impressed observers was the speed of the Prussian mobilization. This was achieved largely thanks to the layout of the railway system, specifically designed with this in mind. The precision of the Prussian Army's movements was also noteworthy, as was the Dreyse needle gun, which, although outranged by the Austrian Lorenz muzzle-loading rifle, could be loaded when prone and had a faster rate of fire. This and the rifle-barrelled cannon used by the Austrians were indicative of the dramatic influence that the Industrial Age was having on weaponry.

The Prussian army had come of age, but that of France was still considered supreme. Furthermore, France was aware of Wilhelm's ultimate objective of combining the German states and was bitterly opposed to it, seeing it as a threat to her own powerful standing in Europe. War between the two became increasingly inevitable. Eventually, in July 1870, an argument broke out over the succession to the Spanish throne. The Spanish accepted the nomination of a Hohenzollern princeling on the proviso that France and Prussia supported it. Wilhelm naturally did, but there were violent objections from the French. Diplomatic misunderstandings and war fever in Paris precipitated the outbreak of hostilities on 19 July.

Both sides began with military advantages. In France's case these were primarily technical. The French Chassepot breech-loading rifle had an effective range of 1200 yards, twice that of the needle gun with which the Prussians were still armed. More significant was Reffeye's *mitrail-*

leuse, a machine gun working on the Gatling principle, which was deployed in such secrecy that the troops did not have a chance to handle it until just a few days before the outbreak of war. Then, with no time to think through the tactical doctrine for its use, they made the mistake of treating it as artillery rather than as an

Above: *King Wilhelm I of Prussia. The war would unite the German states under him as emperor of all Germany.*

Left: *The luckless Marshal Francois-Achille Bazaine. He cut his teeth with the French Foreign Legion in Algeria and Spain, fought with distinction in the Crimean War, and in Napoleon III's eventually disastrous Mexican adventure. His reward for the surrender at Metz would be imprisonment and permanent exile.*

infantry weapon. Hence, its effect was not to be as great as it might have been. The French also continued to place their faith in the mystical *élan* of their soldiers.

The Prussian strengths, apart from their breech-loading artillery, were more organizational. At the heart was the Prussian General Staff, a body which had originally been set up towards the end of the Napoleonic Wars. This team of highly trained staff officers (the Prussian army was the first to conduct formal staff training) had been largely responsible for the success against Denmark and Austria, especially in the swift Prussian mobilization and deployment, and enabled the army, through clear orders and careful coordination between the various formations, to operate like a well-oiled machine. In contrast, the French staff was inexperienced, out of touch with the army, and ill-trained for its task.

It was the Prussian General Staff who had drawn up the plan for the invasion of France. In-deed, they had been working on it for three years. Three armies were formed as follows:

First Army (von Steinmetz) – two corps, one cavalry division (60,000 men)
Second Army (Prince Frederick Charles) – three corps, Guards, two cavalry divisions (131,000 men)
Third Army (Crown Prince) – four corps, two infantry and one cavalry divisions (130,000 men)

In addition, there was a reserve of two corps, comprising 60,000 men under the King of Prussia himself. The Prussian Chief of the General Staff, Count Helmuth von Moltke, the chief architect of the plan, used the principle that the French would be attacked wherever they were found, but that the Prussian armies would be deployed sufficiently close to one another so that he would always have numerical superiority over the French. Consequently, the

Below: The course of the Franco-Prussian War. Although the fighting continued into 1871 the issue was decided once the bulk of the French armies had been trapped with their backs to the frontiers.

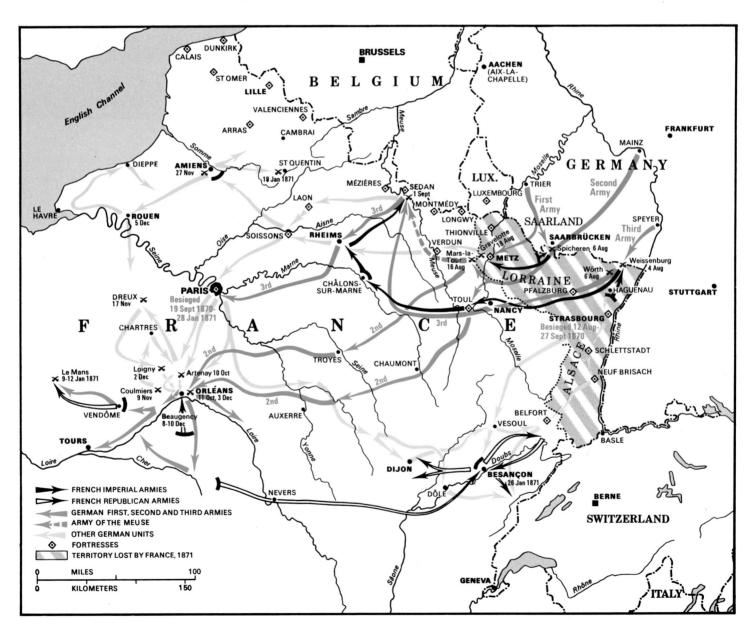

Above: Bavarian troops flush French infantry from a railway embankment.

Far left and left: French infantry in action. Their courage was not in question, but élan *could not compensate for organizational defects.*

Right: *Emperor Napoleon III. Nephew of Napoleon Bonaparte, his efforts to restore France's dominant position in Europe were shattered in 1870.*

Below: *Von Moltke conducting operations at Sedan. Much of the Prussian success is attributable to their highly efficient staff system, something the French lacked.*

armies were initially deployed on a front of 100 miles centered on Saarbrücken and the main axis of advance was to be from here west to Paris.

While the initial German deployment went like clockwork, that of the French was chaotic – a penalty to be paid for their inefficient staff system. It was aggravated by the strategy adopted, which was the brainchild of the Emperor Napoleon III himself. Realizing that the Prussians could mobilize more men, he decided on a pre-emptive attack across the Rhine designed to force the south German states to desert Prussia. He would then march on Austria and, hopefully in combination with her, advance north to Berlin, while his fleet

threatened the Baltic. He was soon forced to abandon this since nothing but confusion reigned while his seven corps struggled to form. Formations found themselves without ammunition and transport and no one had thought to draw up a railway timetable. The corps themselves were scattered over a wide area and, in order to try and institute some organization, Napoleon ordered them to be formed into two armies, one around Strasbourg under Marshal MacMahon and the other commanded by Marshal Bazaine and based on Metz. The Emperor himself exercised overall command.

By the end of July the French corps were still not complete, but the clamor of the Paris mob for action forced Napoleon into ordering Bazaine to advance into Saarland. The Prussian reaction was to initially give ground so that their First and Second Armies could unite to face this threat, while the Third Army crossed the frontier in order to prevent MacMahon linking up with Bazaine. This precipitated the first major clash of the war, at Wörth on 6 August. The Prussian Crown Prince's Army did not perform as well as might have been expected, displaying lack of coordination in its attacks. Nevertheless, its numbers were sufficient to force MacMahon to withdraw, firstly to Neufchâteau and then, once the threat to Paris became clear, by rail to Châlons.

In the meantime, there was a skirmish at Saarbrücken on 2 August. This was occupied by the French for a brief time before they withdrew their forward troops to a less exposed position at Spicheren to the southwest. Here on the 5th the Prussians attacked and persuaded the French to withdraw. This reverse and that at Wörth initiated a panic order for both French armies to fall back on Châlons. Fears of an uprising in Paris then caused Napoleon to rescind it on the 9th, but while Bazaine conformed to this, MacMahon, his troops now moving by rail, did not. Thus the French armies were now separated by some 90 miles. In contrast, the Prussians, who had now begun their main advance into France, were concentrated and moving towards Bazaine, who had been ordered to defend Metz at all costs.

On 12 August, his health failing him and under increasing criticism from Paris, Napoleon handed over executive command to Bazaine. His first step was to abandon Metz because it lacked sufficient supplies and to fall back to Verdun and the River Meuse. The Prussian threat was growing, however, and there was a danger that an enveloping movement from the south could cut Bazaine off from Verdun. Eventually, the Prussians managed to get astride the Metz-Verdun road at Vionville, and the following day, 16 August, was fought the Battle of Mars-la-Tour. Each side lost some

Above: *French marines desperately trying to hold back I Bavarian Corps on the Douzy road, 1 September 1870, the day of crisis at Sedan.*

Above: *Prussian infantry, wearing the* pickelhaube *helmet, driving the French back from the outskirts of Sedan.*

16,000 men and it was a tactical draw. However, it forced Bazaine to give up all ideas of withdrawing to Verdun. Instead he retraced his footsteps and took up position to the northwest of Metz. He was therefore placing himself with his back to the German frontier. During this operation Colonel Ardant du Picq was mortally wounded by a shell while at the head of his regiment. The Prussians followed up, also with their backs to the French base, and on the 18th engaged Bazaine at Gravelotte. A total of 40,000 casualties resulted before Bazaine's flank was turned and he was left with no option but to withdraw inside the fortress of Metz.

The Prussians had not calculated on a major French force holding Metz and had to carry out a hasty reorganization. The whole of First Army and the bulk of the Second were combined under Prince Frederick Charles to keep Bazaine tied down, while the Third Army and a new Army of the Meuse under the Crown Prince of Saxony were ordered to advance on Paris. Likewise, the French, too, formed a new army, the Army of Châlons, under MacMahon. Many of its 130,000 members were raw recruits, who had to be hastily taught how to fire their rifles.

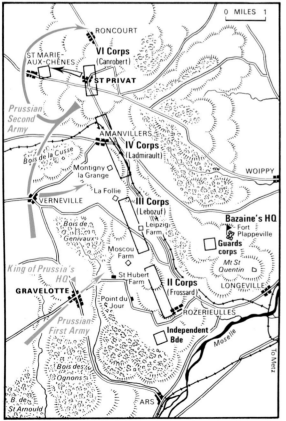

Above: *Another view of the street fighting in the southern suburbs of Sedan on 1 September 1870.*

Left: *The Battle of St Gravelotte, 18 August 1870. When the Germans succeeded in turning Bazaine's right flank at St Privat he had no other option than to withdraw to Metz.*

MacMahon's original intention was to retire on Reims, which he began to do on 21 August. But then word came from Paris that the Emperor's position was in jeopardy and that there would be grave consequences if MacMahon left Bazaine in the lurch. Simultaneously Bazaine sent a message to him saying that he intended to withdraw northwards from Metz. MacMahon therefore began to advance northeast towards Montmédy in order to link up with Bazaine. Meanwhile the Crown Prince of Saxony entered a deserted Châlons on the 24th and discovered, much to his surprise, since it left the way to Paris open, that MacMahon was now at Reims and intending to relieve Metz. Orders were therefore given by von Moltke for his two armies to swing north in order to prevent this. Bazaine now changed his mind, considering that the risk of destruction of his army was greater in open country than in the fortifications of Metz. MacMahon therefore decided to withdraw to Mézières, but again, as this was put in train, further orders came from Paris insisting that he continue to Montmédy. Order and counter-order affected his troops and their morale fell sharply. Worse was to follow.

Left: *Another desperate French attempt to stem the tide of disaster at Sedan.*

Below: *Totally surrounded, with confusion over who was in overall command, the fighting at Sedan on 1 September could only have one result for the French defenders.*

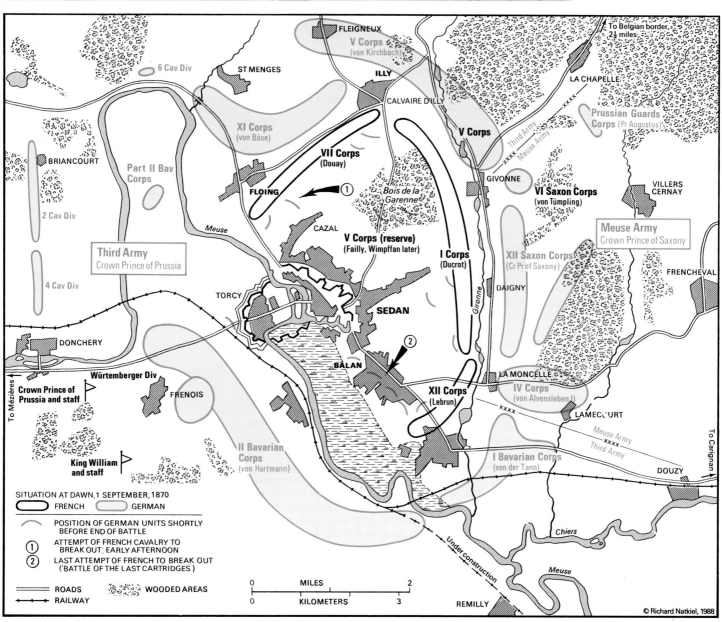

FLEIGNEUX

V Corps
(von Kirchbach)

To Belgian border,
2½ miles

6 Cav Div

ST MENGES

ILLY

CALVAIRE D'ILLY

LA CHAPELLE

XI Corps
(von Böse)

V Corps

Third Army
Meuse Army

Prussian Guards
Corps (Pr Augustus)

BRIANCOURT

Part II Bav
Corps

VII Corps
(Douay)

①

GIVONNE

VI Saxon Corps
(von Tümpling)

VILLERS
CERNAY

2 Cav Div

FLOING

Bois de la
Garenne

Meuse Army
Crown Prince of Saxony

Meuse

CAZAL

V Corps (reserve)
(Failly, Wimpffan later)

I Corps
(Ducrot)

XII Saxon Corps
(Cr Pr of Saxony)

FRENCHEVAL

Third Army
Crown Prince of Prussia

4 Cav Div

Givonne

DAIGNY

TORCY

SEDAN

Württemberger Div

DONCHERY

Crown Prince of
Prussia and staff

FRENOIS

BALAN

②

LA MONCELLE

IV Corps
(von Alvensleben II)

To Mézières

XII Corps
(Lebrun)

LAMECOURT

King William
and staff

II Bavarian
Corps
(von Hartmann)

I Bavarian Corps
(von der Tann)

Meuse Army
Third Army

DOUZY

To Carignan

SITUATION AT DAWN, 1 SEPTEMBER, 1870
☐ FRENCH   ☐ GERMAN

Under construction

Chiers

POSITION OF GERMAN UNITS SHORTLY
BEFORE END OF BATTLE

① ATTEMPT OF FRENCH CAVALRY TO
BREAK OUT: EARLY AFTERNOON

② LAST ATTEMPT OF FRENCH TO BREAK OUT
('BATTLE OF THE LAST CARTRIDGES')

ROADS   WOODED AREAS

RAILWAY

0   MILES   2

0   KILOMETERS   3

REMILLY

Meuse

© Richard Natkiel, 1988

On 30 August the Crown Prince of Saxony's troops surprised one of MacMahon's corps while they were watering their horses and drawing rations. The French were driven back with the loss of 4800 men and 42 guns. As a result MacMahon decided that a link up with Bazaine was no longer possible and that he would withdraw to Sedan, close to the Belgian frontier, commenting, 'This has been an unfortunate day.' Even so, believing that the Prussians opposing him only had 60-70,000 men, he still thought that he could beat them and 'drive them into the Meuse'. As for von Moltke, the way ahead was clear; the French were to be squeezed between the Meuse and the Belgian frontier and he was quite prepared to ignore Belgian neutrality in order to disarm them.

On 31 August the French began to fall back into the fortress of Sedan. The Emperor Napoleon also arrived here at the same time. Sedan itself was in an even worse state with regard to supplies than Metz. With only 200,000 rations stocked there the army could not expect to remain there long. Not that MacMahon intended to, being determined to attack. During that same day the Prussians began to force crossings over the Meuse, a task made easier by the fact that the French engineers were left, because of the growing confusion, without the means to demolish the bridges. Thus, although the French were initially successful in driving the attackers back, they still held the bridges at the end of the day. The morrow, though, would decide the issue, but as one French soldier wrote home: 'Eve of Jena, or eve of Waterloo, which? God alone knows.'

1 September 1870 dawned foggy down on the Meuse, but the Prussians were on the move early. Saxons and Bavarians crossed the Meuse east of Sedan separately at 4am and penetrated some distance before being driven back, but the Saxon artillery was able to silence the French guns opposite it. There now occurred a bizarre event, but, on the other hand, typical of the confusion which had dogged the French high command throughout the campaign. At about 7am MacMahon was wounded by artillery fire and ordered General Ducrot, one of the corps commanders, to succeed him. He had been against giving battle at Sedan and had been watching the enemy columns advance. He now gave orders for a withdrawal towards Mézières to his own I Corps and Lebrun's XII Corps, who were both just to the south of Sedan. The corps to the north of them was commanded by General de Wimpffen. He had been summoned from commanding the French forces at Oran in Algeria on 22 August by the recently appointed prime minister, General Count Palikao. On arrival in Paris he was told to take over V Corps, but was also given a letter written by Palikao which

Above: *The French Imperial Guard tries to rally. (Painting by Albert David, 1896.)*

Right: *Surrender negotiations, Sedan, night 1/2 September 1870. The French defeat left the way to Paris wide open.*

de Wimpfen

de Moltke

35. SEDAN-DONCHERY

from now we shall have thrust the enemy into the Meuse', he told him.

By now it was 10.30am and the situation had developed dramatically. The Prussian Third Army had crossed the Meuse west of Sedan at Donchéry, swung right to the north of the fortress and linked up with the Army of the Meuse, which was advancing from the east of Sedan. The French were now totally surrounded and were being pounded by the Prussian artillery. De Wimpffen does not seem to have realized what had happened, but Ducrot did and ordered Marguerite's cavalry division to cut a path through the Prussians to the northwest so that he could extricate his corps. The French cavalry made three desperately brave charges, but all ended in failure. De Wimpffen, on the other hand, still believed that he could smash his way through to the south-east, inviting the Emperor to accompany this attack. Napoleon, however, had had enough and ordered a white flag to be hoisted. De Wimpffen refused to accept this and continued to try and rally troops for a counterattack. It was, however, too late; word of the impending surrender had already spread like wild fire. Accusing Ducrot of disobeying his orders, the now distraught de Wimpffen was eventually forced to accept the reality of the situation.

Next morning the Emperor personally surrendered himself to Wilhelm, leaving de Wimpffen to march into captivity at the head of 104,000 men. A further 3000 Frenchmen had been killed and 14,000 wounded. The Prussian losses were some 9000 killed and wounded. It was a devastating victory and determined the result of the war. Within the month Paris was under siege, as were a number of French fortresses, including Metz. All these, apart from Belfort, fell within the next few weeks, the luckless Bazaine surrendering almost 180,000 men at Metz. Finally, on 29 January 1871, Paris capitulated. An event of even greater significance to Wilhelm I took place some days earlier in the Hall of Mirrors at Versailles. He was proclaimed Emperor of Germany and his aim of German unification had been achieved.

The Franco-Prussian War had shown only too starkly that the moral factor, while still important, was not enough to win victory in modern war. Organization and careful planning were just as vital. It also made the Prussian Army the foremost in Europe and other armies, notably the British and American, now adopted the *pickelhaube*, the spiked Prussian helmet, as part of their dress. As for France, it was the end of the Napoleonic dynasty, and the ceding of Alsace and Lorraine to Germany produced deep resentment and a desire for revenge in French hearts. It was a revenge which would eventually come, but at heavy cost.

Top: *A symbolic French painting of the signing of the Treaty of Frankfurt, which formally ended the war, on 10 May 1871. French bitterness, as reflected here, fueled a desire for revenge.*

Above: *In contrast, Wilhelm I had enjoyed his moment of ultimate glory when he was proclaimed Emperor of all Germany in the Hall of Mirrors, Versailles, on 18 January 1871.*

stated that he was to succeed MacMahon should he become incapacitated. When de Wimpffen arrived at Sedan on the eve of the battle, he did not, for some reason show MacMahon this letter. Now hearing of the latter's wound and Ducrot's decision to withdraw, he galloped across to Lebrun, showed him the letter, and ordered him to halt his withdrawal, believing that the repulse of the Bavarians promised a French victory. He then scribbled a note to Ducrot telling him that he was no longer in command. On receipt of this, Ducrot went to see de Wimpffen. While he was horrified at de Wimpffen's ignorance of the geography of the battlefield, which was perhaps not surprising, given his late arrival, he had to accept the authority of the latter. De Wimpffen then went to reassure the Emperor. 'Within two hours

ISANDHLWANA
1879

A significant part of nineteenth century warfare consisted of modern Western armies being employed against native tribes often armed with the most primitive of weapons. Inevitably the white men were vastly outnumbered, but were usually victorious. Occasionally, though, the result was not as expected and when this was so, the shock waves reverberated out of all proportion to the size of the battle which produced them. One example of this was the destruction of George Custer and his US 7th Cavalry by the Sioux Indians at Little Big Horn in June 1876. Another was the British reverse at Isandhlwana in South Africa.

The Zulus are a Bantu tribe and originate from what is now the province of Natal in South Africa. They were notable for their sophisticated, at least by African standards, military organization. Their warriors were conscripted, with all young men being taken to live in military kraals and not being allowed to marry without the king's agreement. They served in regiments which were called *impis* and which varied in strength between 1000 and 2500 men. The impis were manned according to age, although those formed by the younger age groups always had a leavening of veterans. The Zulu warrior's main weapon was the assegai, a form of javelin which came in two types. The longer version was for throwing and had an effective range of 70 yards and he normally carried two of these, together with a shorter type, which was used in close quarter fighting as a stabbing weapon. To protect himself he carried an oxhide shield, which carried the particular identifying mark of his impi, as did his headdress. The fundamental tactic was that of double envelopment. The two wings or horns of the impi first trapped the enemy and then the center or chest moved in for the kill. This was very effective and made all the more so by rigid discipline. The Zulus first came to prominence during the reign of King Chaka in the early part of the nineteenth century. He himself was murdered by his brother Dingaan in 1828. Dingaan, however, eventually fell foul of the Boers. He had promised them a tract of land in return for services rendered, but then went back on his word, massacring the Boers with whom he had been negotiating. The Boers took their revenge and Dingaan was deposed, his half brother becoming king in his place. The British had, however, been gradually colonizing South Africa, fighting a number of wars against the Kaffirs, and in 1843 annexed Natal. In 1852, towards the end of the last of their wars against the Kaffirs, the British agreed with the Boers, who had been driven further into the hinterland as the British presence spread, that they should hold the Orange Free State and the Transvaal as

independent Boer republics. At the same time, the British recognized Zululand and there was peace for the next 25 years.

In 1877, however, the British annexed Transvaal. This was in the belief that South Africa as a whole would be better served if union between the British and the Boers was achieved, but also because gold had been found in the region and the Boers seemed incapable of securing Transvaal both economically and against the native tribes. Appointed in the same year as Governor-General of Cape Colony was Sir Bartle Frere and it was his actions that brought about war with the Zulus.

Their king was now Cetshwayo, who had come to the Zulu throne in 1857 and had been living at peace with his British neighbors in Natal. Frere was concerned to educate the native tribes out of their primitive savagery in order to better combat famine and disease. In particular he wanted to bring the Zulus to heel and saw a way to do this through a territorial dispute between the Boers and Zulus which was inherited with the annexation of Transvaal. Thinking that a boundary commission would find in favor of the British, he obtained Zulu agreement for the matter to be resolved in this way. The commission, to his chagrin, found for the Zulus. He therefore hedged British accep-

Previous pages, main picture: 'The last command we heard was "Fix bayonets and die like English soldiers do".'

Inset: *A Zulu warrior in traditional dress.*

Above: *Lord Chelmsford, commander of the British forces. His and others' gross underestimation of the military capabilities of the Zulus were largely instrumental in the disaster at Isandhlwana.*

Left: *King Cetshwayo being taken by sea to Cape Town after his ultimate defeat at Ulundi, July 1879.*

tance of this with so many conditions and accompanied it with an ultimatum which demanded the disbandment of the Zulu army. He knew that Cetshwayo could not possibly accept this. Eleven days after the expiry of the ultimatum on the last day of 1878, British troops invaded Zululand.

The British commander was Lord Chelmsford, a veteran of the Crimea and the British expedition to Abyssinia in 1868. He saw his objective as the Zulu capital of Ulundi, which was situated in the geographic center of Zululand. The main invasion was to be carried out by three columns. In the extreme east, near the coast, the right hand column would cross the River Tugela and head for Eshowe. The center column would advance by Rorke's Drift and move eastwards to Ulundi, while the left hand column would enter from Utrecht in Transvaal and head southeast to the Zulu capital. Chelmsford himself would move with the center column. He also had two additional elements. One force would cover the Pongola River in the extreme north, while the other was based on Kranz Kop and covered the southern Zulu border. On paper the scheme looked impressive, but had a significant flaw. The three columns initially advancing into Zululand were separated from one another by a considerable distance, which would make co-operation among them very difficult.

In contrast, Cetshwayo had no initial plan. He merely mobilized 27 impis, amounting in all to some 50,000 men and instructed them to en-

gage and destroy the British wherever they met them, but on no account to cross the Zulu borders.

The drama that was about to unfold concerned the center column. This was commanded by Colonel Glyn and was built round two battalions of the 24th Foot (later South Wales Borderers). In addition it had locally raised mounted infantry, a native contingent and an artillery battery. Its strength all told was 1747 European and 2866 native troops. Glyn's troops crossed the frontier on 11 January 1879, leaving a company of the 24th to guard Rorke's Drift, and had their first brush with the Zulus the following day, driving some warriors out of a kraal. A week's inactivity followed while a road

Above: *A Zulu chief and his escort. Although the Zulus had some firearms, their marksmanship was poor and they relied more on the assegai.*

65

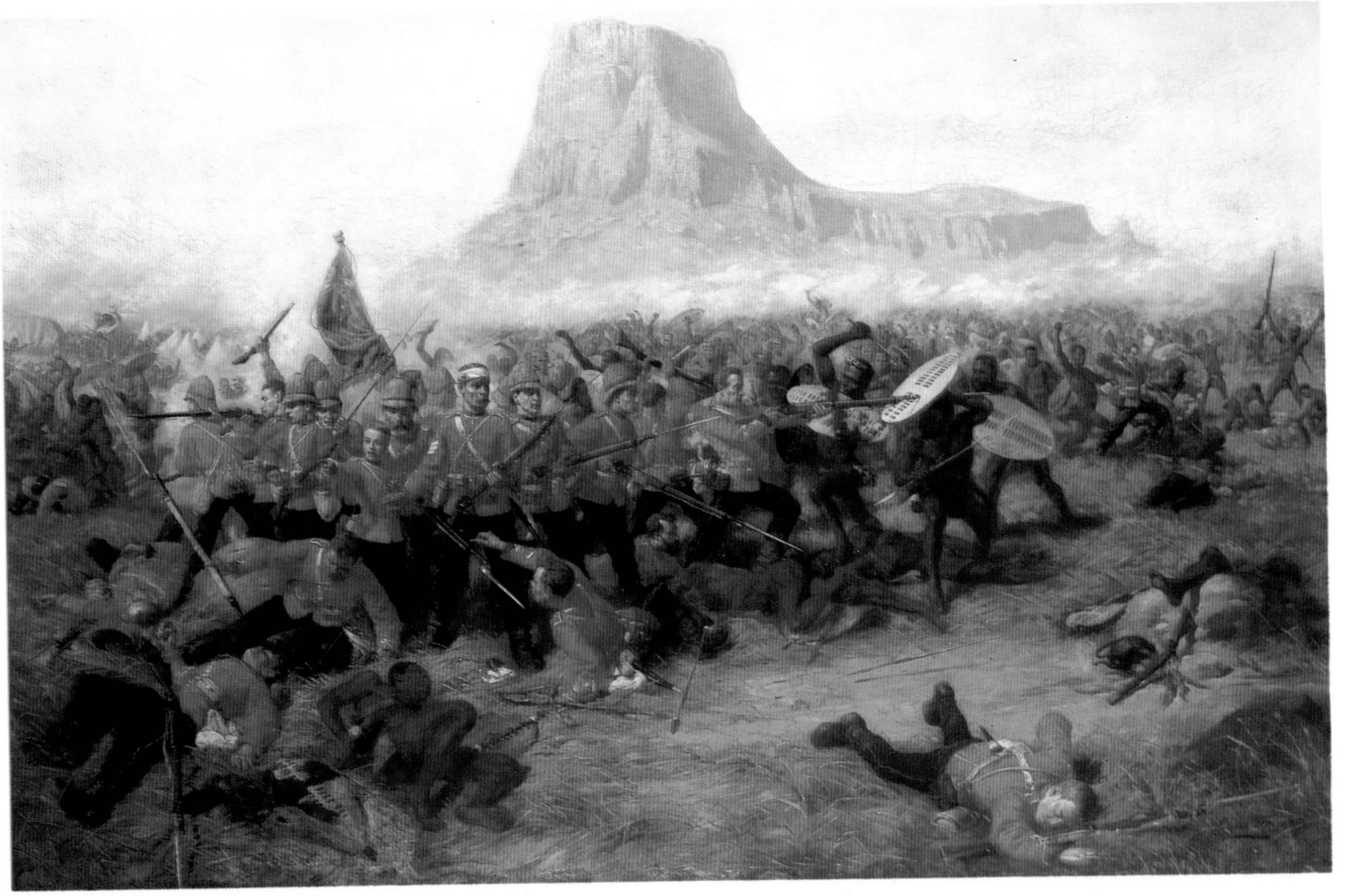

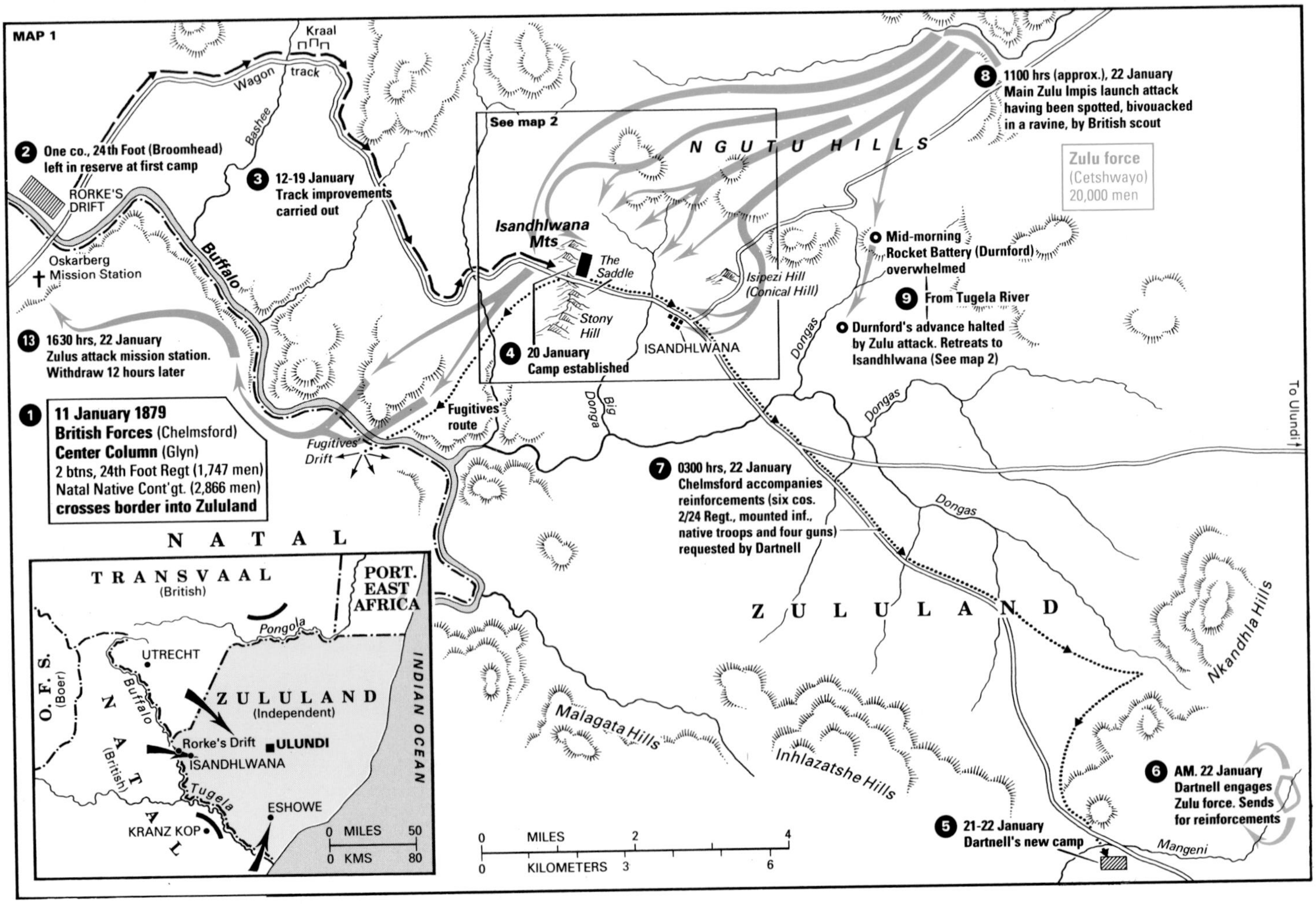
MAP 1
Kraal
Wagon track
Bashee
1 11 January 1879 British Forces (Chelmsford) Center Column (Glyn) 2 btns, 24th Foot Regt (1,747 men) Natal Native Cont'gt. (2,866 men) crosses border into Zululand
2 One co., 24th Foot (Broomhead) left in reserve at first camp
3 12-19 January Track improvements carried out
4 20 January Camp established
5 21-22 January Dartnell's new camp
6 AM. 22 January Dartnell engages Zulu force. Sends for reinforcements
7 0300 hrs, 22 January Chelmsford accompanies reinforcements (six cos. 2/24 Regt., mounted inf., native troops and four guns) requested by Dartnell
8 1100 hrs (approx.), 22 January Main Zulu Impis launch attack having been spotted, bivouacked in a ravine, by British scout
9 From Tugela River
13 1630 hrs, 22 January Zulus attack mission station. Withdraw 12 hours later
Mid-morning Rocket Battery (Durnford) overwhelmed
Durnford's advance halted by Zulu attack. Retreats to Isandhlwana (See map 2)
Zulu force (Cetshwayo) 20,000 men
See map 2
RORKE'S DRIFT
Oskarberg Mission Station
Buffalo
Isandhlwana Mts
The Saddle
Stony Hill
ISANDHLWANA
Isipezi Hill (Conical Hill)
NGUTU HILLS
Fugitives route
Fugitives' Drift
Big Donga
Dongas
To Ulundi
NATAL
ZULULAND
Nkandhla Hills
Malagata Hills
Inhlazatshe Hills
Mangeni
MILES 0 2 4
KILOMETERS 0 3 6
TRANSVAAL (British)
PORT. EAST AFRICA
O. F. S. (Boer)
UTRECHT
Pongola
Buffalo
ZULULAND (Independent)
INDIAN OCEAN
Rorke's Drift
ULUNDI
ISANDHLWANA
NATAL (British)
Tugela
ESHOWE
KRANZ KOP
0 MILES 50
0 KMS 80

Left: *The last stand of the 24th Foot, with Mount Isandhlwana in the background.*

Below left: *The maneuvers that led up to the massacre at Isandhlwana.*

Right: *Lts Melville and Coghill try to save the Queen's Colour of the 1st/24th. They were later awarded posthumous Victoria Crosses.*

Above: *Lord Chelmsford's column returning to Isandhlwana the day after the disaster.*

Above right: *Col Wood's column, which entered Zululand from the northwest, striking camp.*

Right: *Battle of Ulundi, 4 July 1879. In the foreground a corporal of the 17th Lancers attends to his injured horse.*

Above: *Col Glyn hands back the Queen's Colour, found amid the debris at Isandhlwana, to the 24th Foot. The regiment, shortly to be retitled the South Wales Borderers, would carry it until after the First World War.*

was improved so that supply wagons could use it. Chelmsford himself used this time to reconnoiter the next camp site. He selected Isandhlwana Mountain, which rose 500 feet above the surrounding plain and was connected to Stony Hill to its south by a col. To the east of the feature ran a dry donga or riverbed and beyond that a plain. To the north lay the Ngutu Hills. The site of the camp itself was to be the plateau just to the east of the mountain, which could be used to protect the camp.

The new camp was established on 20 January, but seems to have been done so in a lax manner. Boers with experience of fighting the Zulus had advised Chelmsford to ensure that camp sites were properly fortified, but no attempt was made to do this, even though he had reports of a Zulu stronghold to the southeast. This Chelmsford personally went to check up on on the 20th, but found nothing. The following morning he despatched three well armed detachments to try and locate this stronghold. In the afternoon Chelmsford received reports from one of these groups that a large force of Zulus had been

spotted in the Malagata Hills, which lay to the south of Isandhlwana. Two of the groups intended to camp out overnight in order to keep track of the Zulus and they requested food and blankets. Early on the morning of the 22nd, though, one of the group commanders, Major Dartnell, sent a message to say that the Zulus were in greater numbers than he first thought and that he urgently needed reinforcement. Chelmsford acceded to this and six companies of the 2/24th, mounted infantry and native troops, accompanied by four guns set out to join Dartnell. Chelmsford also went with this contingent since he wished to select the next camp site.

Lieutenant Colonel Pulleine was left in charge at Isandhlwana. Under him were seven companies of the 24th Foot, two guns, and some native troops. However, in response to orders from Chelmsford, they were joined shortly before 10am by a rocket battery and additional native troops, which had been sent up by the column watching the Tugela River. Colonel Durnford, the column commander, came with them. In the meantime, Dartnell became engaged in a running fight with the Zulus in the hills to the south. These turned out to be not in the strength that Dartnell had earlier believed, but Chelmsford remained convinced that they represented the main body. Consequently, when he received a message from Pulleine to say that Zulus had been spotted in the Ngutu Hills to the north, Chelmsford did not pay too much attention to it. Instead, at midday, with Dartnell and the reinforcements having been unable to corner the Zulus which they had been chasing, he ordered them back, intending to move on to the next camp site.

Back at Isandhlwana, the garrison had stood to when the first reports of Zulus to the north had been received, which had been at 8am. When Durnford arrived, he took command by virtue of seniority and took his own men, including the rocket battery, to both check to the north and in the plain to the east. As an additional precaution, he also ordered one company of the 1/24th to occupy high ground 1500 yards north of the camp. This done, the remainder of the garrison stood down.

Durnford himself, with two troops of mounted Basutos, a native infantry company, and the rocket battery moved out and round to the south of Conical Hill, which was four miles east of Isandhlwana. As he did so he saw, to his amazement, a large Zulu force on the plain beyond, with a further large body moving round to the north. The Zulus immediately attacked, overwhelming the rocket battery. Durnford and the remainder withdrew to the dry donga east of the camp. By now it was 12.30pm and the camp at Isandhlwana was about to be engulfed.

Pulleine first heard of the danger from the Basuto troop which Durnford had sent to the north. This was close by the detached company of the 24th and Pulleine decided to send two other companies of the 24th up to reinforce them and prevent the right horn of the Zulu force from reaching the camp. The remainder he stood to again.

The troops in the north held the Zulus for a while, but then were forced back by sheer weight of numbers. In the south Durnford battled against the left horn. This soon threatened to cut off his retreat and he had to leave the comparative safety of the river bed and pulled back to Stony Hill. By this time his native infantry had fled, but the Basutos continued to fight for him. Now the center of the Zulu force began to attack the camp itself. For a time the defense not only held, but inflicted fearful punishment on the Zulus. Nevertheless, they continued to attack and after a while ammunition began to run short.

It was at this time, about 1pm, that Chelmsford, now at the new camping ground, which was some 11 miles from Isandhlwana, was first made aware of what was happening. A mounted native told him that artillery fire could be heard in the direction of Isandhlwana. He and his staff immediately rode up to some high ground from which the camp could be seen. They did not consider that the situation was too serious since the tents had not been struck; there had been, in truth, no time to do this. Nevertheless, leaving Colonel Glyn in charge at the new camp site, he decided to ride back to Isandhlwana with a small detachment.

At Isandhlwana the situation had now become critical since the available supply waggons, situated a few hundred yards to the rear, contained little in the way of reserve stocks of ammunition. Thus the volume of fire from the defenders began to die away and this gave the Zulus fresh heart. They got within assegai-throwing range and at this point the native infantry broke and ran. Then it was a matter of bayonet versus short assegai, but the numbers of the latter were too great. It was all over by 2.30pm. A few did manage to escape the carnage, including Lieutenant Horace Smith-Dorrien, who was on the staff of Colonel Glyn's column and 35 years later would be commanding one of the two corps of the British Expeditionary Force in France. It was, however, precious few and 1329 of their comrades had

Above: *Burying the dead at Isandhlwana, an engraving from the* Illustrated London News, *July 1879.*

Above: *The relief of the garrison at Rorke's Drift. A detailed view of the action.*

Opposite: *The gallant defense of Rorke's Drift, which was some compensation for the disaster at Isandhlwana.*

Below: *A detailed study of the action at Isandhlwana.*

perished, together with something over 2000 Zulus.

Chelmsford, even if he immediately realized how desperate the situation was, could not have arrived in time. As it was, he moved slowly since the horses were tired after what had already been a long day for them. As he did so, various messages reached him telling of the grave situation at Isandhlwana. Eventually an officer appeared to say that the camp was in Zulu hands. He himself had earlier ridden to Isandhlwana to arrange for supplies for the native troops and it was only when he got close to the

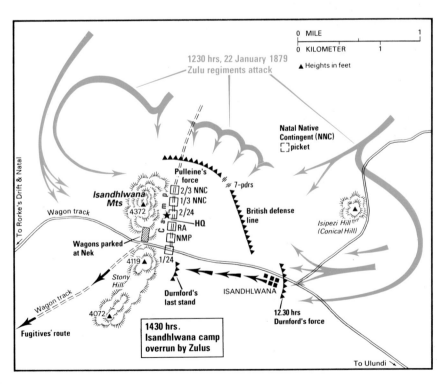

To Rorke's Drift & Natal

0 MILE 1
0 KILOMETER 1
▲ Heights in feet

1230 hrs, 22 January 1879
Zulu regiments attack

Natal Native
Contingent (NNC)
☐ picket

Pulleine's force
☐ 2/3 NNC
☐ 1/3 NNC
☐ 2/24
☐ RA — HQ
☐ NMP

7-pdrs

British defense line

Isandhlwana Mts
4372 ▲

Wagon track

Wagons parked at Nek
4119 ▲
Stony Hill
1/24

Durnford's last stand

Isipezi Hill (Conical Hill)
▲

ISANDHLWANA

Wagon track

4072 ▲

Fugitives' route

12.30 hrs
Durnford's force

1430 hrs.
Isandhlwana camp
overrun by Zulus

To Ulundi ↘

camp that he realized the fate that had befallen it. Chelmsford therefore sent word back to Glyn for him to bring his men up as quickly as possible. He also sent some mounted infantry forward to obtain the latest situation at Isandhlwana. Glyn reacted quickly and had joined Chelmsford by 6.30pm. The force then advanced towards the camp, intent on retaking it from the Zulus. They had, however, abandoned it, but fires seen in the area indicated that they were still about. Chelmsford therefore halted his force short of the camp and adopted a position of all-round defense for the night. At this stage he still believed that at least a portion of the force at Isandhlwana had withdrawn to Rorke's Drift. He assumed this despite the large number of corpses visible in the dark that indicated casualties had been high. Between 10pm and midnight, however, a bright light and sounds of firing from the direction of Rorke's Drift indicated that it, too, was under attack. Chelmsford's men were too tired to do anything about it immediately and, indeed, it would have been foolish to move from their position in the dark.

What in fact had happened, was that of the

14,000 Zulus which had been directed on Isandhlwana, 4000 had been sent on to Rorke's Drift. This, as has been related earlier, was defended by a company of the 24th Foot, commanded by Lieutenant Bromhead, and a few other individuals; in all, 139 men under command of an engineer officer, Lieutenant Chard. They took up position around the Oskarberg mission station, which enabled them to cover the drift (or ford) across the River Buffalo. The Zulus approached at 4.30pm, some two hours after the last resistance at Isandhlwana had ceased. There followed 12 hours of intense action, as wave after wave of Zulus attacked, some penetrating the makeshift stockade. The defenders managed to hold out and eventually the Zulus drew off, leaving 350 of their number dead. The defense suffered 17 killed and ten wounded. This gallant action went some way to counterbalancing Isandhlwana, but could not conceal the fact that the latter was a disaster.

Indeed, Isandhlwana brought a halt to offensive operations for the time being. The morale

Below: Cetshwayo as portrayed by the famous Victorian cartoonist Spy.

Above: *The 17th Lancers pursue the Zulus after the victory at Ulundi, by C E Fripp.*

of the native troops in the British service had plummeted and four battalions had to be disbanded and reinforcements brought up. The left hand column, operating in the north, had made little progress, while that on the right was shut up in Eshowe, which it reached on 23 January, being eventually relieved in April. The center column, meanwhile, was withdrawn to Helpmakaar west of the Buffalo River in order to reorganize. Chelmsford himself offered to resign, but this was not immediately taken up by the British Government, although they did eventually select another commander, one of the most famous of Victorian soldiers, Sir Garnet Wolseley.

It was not until June, after substantial reinforcements had arrived, that Chelmsford was able to resume his invasion. In the meantime the northern column, which was camped at Mount Kambula, had, in March, suffered two minor reverses, but also a significant success when its camp came under heavy Zulu attack. Chelmsford's force now consisted of 17,500 men, split into two divisions. The 1st Division marched up the coast, without meeting any Zulus, to Port Durnford, while the 2nd Division struck at Ulundi from Dundee. It was here on 4 July that the final battle was fought when Cetshwayo's Zulus flung themselves time and again at a square formed from 5000 men and supported by 12 artillery and a number of machine guns. They were massacred, while the British losses were a mere 12 killed and 88 wounded. Cetshwayo himself was captured six weeks later, reinstated, but only to be deposed in a civil war. Nevertheless, he lived until 1894 when he died at Ekowe.

While Chelmsford had succeeded in achieving the object of the campaign before Wosleley arrived, much to the latter's annoyance, the stigma of Isandhlwana remained with him and he received no further advancement. The truth was that he had been too complacent and it was this that had cost the lives of so many of his men. Underestimation of the enemy is a recurring military sin.

TSUSHIMA STRAITS

1905

The Russo-Japanese War (1904-5) is signficant for a number of reasons. One was that the war on land, especially around Port Arthur, provided an accurate forecast of the trench warfare of 1914-18. Another, and even more important, was that it was the culmination of Japan's program, begun in the 1860s, of adopting Western technology to make herself a world power. This manifested itself most dramatically in the rise of the Imperial Japanese Navy.

When the American Commodore Matthew Perry visited Japan in 1853 with his squadron of four steamships he little imagined what effect it would have on this secretive and static society. Indeed, it resulted in 15 years of civil strife between those who wanted to progress into the nineteenth century and those who regarded any Western influence as an anathema. It was the progressives who eventually came out on top in

Previous pages: *A Japanese impression of the Battle of Tsushima.*

Right: *The Japanese fleet opens fire at Tsushima.*

1868, with the Emperor adopting the name *Meiji* or 'Enlightened Rule'. One of the immediate results of this was the disbanding of the private fleets of the warlords, and the creation of a national navy, which, in 1872 became a department of state.

The Japanese had noted with intense interest the introduction of ironclads into Western navies and were determined to replace their motley collection of wooden schooners with them. Recognizing that Britain's navy ruled the waves, it was here that their delegations visited and ordered modern warships. The navy's first test came in 1894 during the war with China. On 17 September a Japanese squadron of 12 ships clashed with a Chinese squadron of similar size in Korea Bay in the northern part of the Yellow Sea. After five hours of canonnading, five Chinese ships had been sunk while the Japanese

squadron was still intact. The world was impressed and the renowned American naval strategist Captain A T Mahan was moved to comment that the Imperial Japanese Navy would soon be one of the most powerful. It would, however, be only a few years before it was next put to the test.

The root cause of the Russo-Japanese War was rivalry among the major powers over China. Initially, in the mid-nineteenth century, it had been Britain, France and Germany who led the way, forcing the weak Chinese government to grant them concessions. The Russians then became involved and so too did the Japanese. During the Sino-Japanese War of 1894 the Japanese had seized Port Arthur in Manchuria, but had been forced by the major powers to hand it over to Russia. In compensation Japan received Formosa, but the loss of Port Arthur rankled, especially when the Russians began to construct the Trans-Siberian railway in order to consolidate their hold on it. Worse was to follow. Japan considered Korea to be in her sphere of influence as a result of her successful war against China. She discovered, however, that the Russians were planning not only to secure Manchuria for themselves, but to also bring Korea under their influence. The Japanese offered to respect Russia's position in Manchuria if the Russians would do the same over Korea. The Russians, however, won timber concessions in northern Korea and, in order to safeguard these, sent troops there and decided to strengthen their naval and land forces in Manchuria. Foiled in her attempt at diplomatic resolution of the problem, Japan decided that force was the only answer.

Since Port Arthur was the main cause of Japanese discontent, it was this that they decided to attack. It could only be effectively tackled from the landward side, but in order to deploy troops here the threat of the Russian Eastern Fleet must be removed. This had to be done quickly since it was known that the Russians intended to reinforce with their Baltic Fleet and this would give them overwhelming naval superiority over the Japanese. The plan they drew up was for a surprise attack, which was in many ways to be reflected by that against Pearl Harbor nearly 40 years later. On the night 8/9 February 1904 Japanese torpedo boats attacked Russian ships, sinking three. Next day the Russian fleet engaged the Japanese in an indecisive action, but the Japanese were sufficiently successful to force the Russians on to the defensive. Simultaneously, Japanese troops landed near Seoul in Korea and began to advance north towards Manchuria. It was only then that Japan formally declared war.

The Japanese First Army soon drove the Russians out of northern Korea and in May two

Above: *Russian shore batteries repulsing a Japanese naval attack at Port Arthur, which was under siege from June 1904 until January 1905.*

Left: *Admiral Zinovi Rozhdestvenski and the Russian Consul at Tangiers when the Baltic Fleet called in there during its long voyage east.*

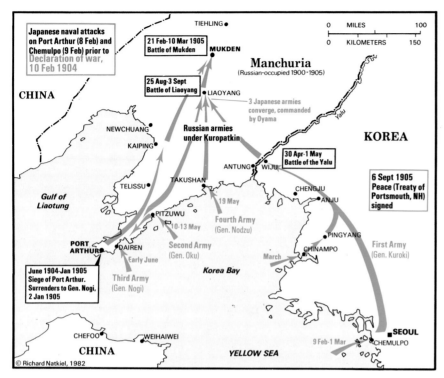

Japanese naval attacks on Port Arthur (8 Feb) and Chemulpo (9 Feb) prior to Declaration of war, 10 Feb 1904

21 Feb-10 Mar 1905 Battle of Mukden

25 Aug-3 Sept Battle of Liaoyang

30 Apr-1 May Battle of the Yalu

6 Sept 1905 Peace (Treaty of Portsmouth, NH) signed

June 1904-Jan 1905 Siege of Port Arthur. Surrenders to Gen. Nogi, 2 Jan 1905

TIEHLING
MUKDEN
Manchuria
(Russian-occupied 1900-1905)
CHINA
LIAOYANG
3 Japanese armies converge, commanded by Oyama
NEWCHUANG
KAIPING
Russian armies under Kuropatkin
KOREA
ANTUNG WIJU
Yalu
CHENGJU
Gulf of Liaotung
TELISSU
TAKUSHAN
19 May
ANJU
PITZUWU
10-13 May
Fourth Army (Gen. Nodzu)
PINGYANG
First Army (Gen. Kuroki)
PORT ARTHUR
DAIREN
Second Army (Gen. Oku)
Early June
CHINAMPO
Korea Bay
March
Third Army (Gen. Nogi)
CHEFOO
WEIHAIWEI
SEOUL
9 Feb-1 Mar
CHEMULPO
CHINA
YELLOW SEA

© Richard Natkiel, 1982

MILES 0 100
KILOMETERS 0 150

Above: *Japanese land operations during the war with Russia.*

Above right: *Contemporary Japanese painting of a gun crew in action.*

Right: *The Russian fleet in battle formation.*

Far right: *The long voyage of the Russian Baltic Fleet to its graveyard in the Tsushima Straits.*

further armies were landed in Manchuria, west of the Yalu River and well to the north of Port Arthur. These combined with the First Army in an advance towards Mukden. Finally, in June another army was landed just north of Port Arthur and began to lay siege to it. Matters went from bad to worse for the Russians as the Japanese armies moved remorselessly north towards Mukden and Port Arthur remained tightly sealed. In Moscow it seemed that the only hope of salvation lay in the mighty Baltic Fleet.

It was not, however, until 15 October 1904 that this fleet, now renamed the Second Pacific Squadron, set sail from the Baltic under the command of Admiral Zinovi Rozhdestvenski. Indecision over whether to send it, and a wish to wait for four new battleships to be commissioned had accounted for the delays. It was an impressive force of almost 50 ships, but they were a disparate collection. Some were so old as to be mechanically unreliable, while the newest had not completed their sea going trials. The officers and men who manned them also left much to be desired. The former generally showed little interest in their profession, while the latter were conscripted from the peasantry and few had even seen the sea before they became sailors. Another major problem was that of keeping their ships supplied with coal in what would be a 20,000 mile voyage. Britain, recognizing the growing potential with Japan and acknowledging the respect in which the Japanese held the Royal Navy, had signed a defensive pact with her in 1902. This meant that since most of the coaling stations en route were British they would be barred to the Russians.

Consequently refueling had to take place at sea and coal was crammed into the ships to such a degree that every available space had to be used, which did little for living conditions. Worse, it made the ships top heavy and this severely affected their handling. Indeed, within a few minutes of weighing anchor one battleship had run aground and another had been rammed by a torpedo boat.

Worse was to follow. On entering the North Sea, the Russian ships came upon some British fishing boats in fog off the Dogger Bank. Convinced, for some reason, that Japanese torpedo boats were lurking among them, the Russians opened fire, sinking some.

It was intensely embarrassing diplomatically, with the Russians being forced to make a formal apology and pay out a large sum of money in compensation. On reaching the Mediterranean, Rozhdestvenski sent his slower, more elderly ships through it and the Suez Canal while he took the remainder round the Cape of Good Hope. The longer the ships were at sea, the

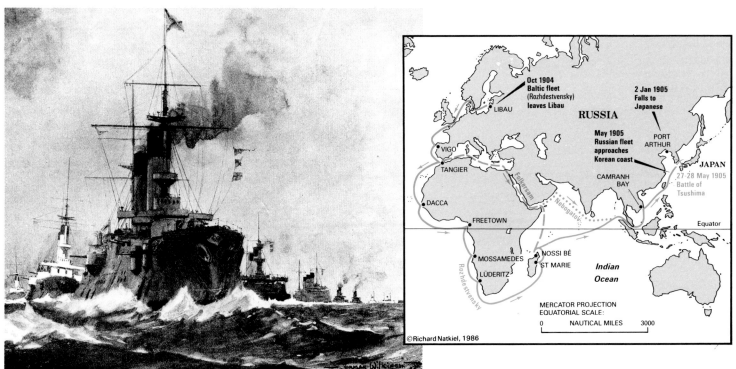

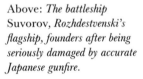

Above: *The battleship* Suvorov, *Rozhdestvenski's flagship, founders after being seriously damaged by accurate Japanese gunfire.*

Above right: *The Russian fleet's embarrassing clash with British trawlers in the North Sea. It was just one of many mishaps.*

lower morale became, and off Madagascar he had to quell the beginnings of a mutiny.

Then came the news that Port Arthur had capitulated on 2 January 1905. With no prospect of early relief, sickness growing, and food stocks becoming very low the garrison had no option. It meant, though, that the Eastern Fleet, which Rozhdestvenski was supposed to link up with, was now largely destroyed. Accordingly, in gloomy mood, he signaled the Russian Admiralty: 'I have not the slightest prospect of recovering command of the sea with the force under my orders. The despatch of reinforcements composed of untested and in some cases badly built vessels would only render the fleet more vulnerable. In my view the only course is to use all force to break through to Vladivostock and from this base to threaten the enemy's communications.' This was accepted and the fleet continued to steam through the Indian Ocean, as yet undetected by the Japanese.

The most direct route to Vladivostock passed through the Tsushima Straits, which separate Japan from Korea, and it was this that Rozhdestvenski decided to take. Accordingly he despatched his colliers to Shanghai, entering the China Sea himself on 9 May. By now Admiral

Togo Heihachiro, commanding the Japanese Main Fleet, was aware of the approaching presence of the Russian fleet and deduced that they would pass through the Tsushima Straits. He therefore deployed 16 ships to cover the entrance to the Straits. He received news of the arrival of the Russian colliers at Shanghai on

Above: *The Japanese fleet steaming to intercept the Russians in the Tsushima Straits.*

Left: *The Russian 2nd Pacific Squadron set sail from Canranh Bay, Indo-China, on the last leg of its fateful voyage.*

taking a more roundabout route, perhaps east of the Japanese mainland and up through the Kuriles or even between the two largest Japanese islands. As midnight passed a fog descended, drastically reducing visibility and making the task of the picquet ships that much more difficult. The Russians, on the other hand, were delighted since it would enable them to slip through the Straits without being spotted. Their optimism was, however, to be shortlived.

At 2.45am the converted merchant cruiser *Shinano Maru* detected navigation lights. She moved towards and shadowed them, unable in the fog to detect what ship they belonged to. As the sky began to lighten she could be identified as an unarmed Russian hospital ship. A few minutes later, as dawn broke, the mist parted and the Japanese crew saw some ten Russian ships under a mile away, as well as the smoke of several others. The Russians had finally arrived, but were aware that they had been spotted.

The *Shinano Maru* immediately signaled Togo, who was in Chinhae Bay, 150 miles from the Russian fleet. She then lost sight of the Russians, apart from one brief glimpse of them. This, however, was sufficient for the armored cruiser *Izumo* to take over the shadowing role at 6.45am. Togo, who had now weighed anchor, decided to head for Okinoshima Island, east of Tsushima Island. Wireless reports from the *Izumo* and other armored cruisers kept him in touch with Russian progress. This indicated indecision. Initially, Rozhdestvenski had been steaming in two parallel lines, but, sighting the shadowing Japanese cruisers, he ordered his ships into a single line, a maneuver that took some time to complete. To his fury one of his ships fired a 12-inch shell at one of the shadowing cruisers, which was a good five miles away, and the other ships joined in. The Japanese merely withdrew to a safer distance, but the Russian crews believed that they had frightened them off and went happily to their dinners. Rozhdestvenski now changed his mind and ordered his ships into line abreast. This was only half completed when the Japanese cruisers reappeared, and so he tried to revert to line ahead. Such was the confusion that the end result was two lines, with the starboard one slightly ahead, but not enough to avoid each column masking the other's guns.

It was shortly after 1.30pm that Togo and the main body sighted the Russians. He immediately altered course to cross ahead of the opposing fleet, what was termed 'crossing the T' and ran up a signal flag on his flagship the *Mikasa*. An echo of Nelson's famous signal at Trafalgar 100 years earlier, it read: 'The fate of the empire depends on this battle. Let every man do his utmost.' Two more turns by the highly drilled Japanese ships into line and

the afternoon of 25 May and expected the Russian fleet itself to appear on the following day.

Throughout 26 May the Japanese waited anxiously, but there were no sightings of the Russian ships. Togo began to worry that he had guessed wrong and that the Russians were

steaming parallel and in the same direction as the Russians, and on their port side. Fire was now opened and was to continue for two hours. The superiority of the Japanese gunnery soon began to tell, the Russians being further disadvantaged by the fact that many of their shells failed to explode. When fog separated the two fleets the Russians had lost the battleship *Oslyabya* and the flagship *Suvorov* had been seriously damaged.

The Russians continued on their way towards Vladivostok and, the fog lifting once more, Togo was able to engage them again in the late afternoon. His gunfire forced the Russians to withdraw into the fog once more, but Togo was able to engage them again before darkness fell. This time two more battleships were sunk, the *Suvorov* was also now at the bottom of the sea and the luckless Rozhdestvenski wounded. He was, however, rescued by Admiral Nebogatov in the battleship *Beduivy.* Nebogatov assumed command and the fleet continued northwards.

Togo, concerned that his battleships were vulnerable to torpedo attack during the hours of darkness, withdrew them and ordered his torpedo boats to continue the action. They were successful in sinking three more Russian ships at the cost of three of theirs. At daybreak the Russians found Togo's main body once more about to engage them. With most of his battleships now sunk, while the Japanese had their four battleships and eight cruisers still in fighting order, Nebogatov realized that to continue to fight would only result in more Russian losses. He therefore ran up the white flag.

Of the 38 ships of the Baltic Fleet which sailed into the Tsushima Straits in the early hours of 27 May, 19 lay at the bottom of the sea. A further seven were captured and six interned in neutral ports. One escaped to Madagascar, leaving just one cruiser and two destroyers to struggle into Vladivostock with the grim news. It was a disaster of major proportions and marked the final nail in the Russian coffin, the major land objective of Mukden having fallen to the Japanese in early March. It was, however, not the Russians who now sued for peace. America stepped in and arranged a negotiated peace which was sealed by the Treaty of Portsmouth on 29 August 1905. By this Russia agreed to evacuate Manchuria, hand over the Liaotung Peninsula, including Port Arthur, and the southern half of Sakhalin Island to the Japanese, as well as recognizing that Korea was in the Japanese sphere of influence. Thus Japan had gained all that she went to war for, but many were dissatisfied. The truth was that the war had almost bankrupted her and she had been hoping for a large indemnity which was not forthcoming.

It was this discontent that may have brought about the loss of Togo's flagship within two weeks of the formal end of the war. The *Misaba* was moored in Sasebo harbor and on the night 11/12 September blew up at her moorings causing 590 casualties among her crew. Togo himself had only gone ashore a few hours before. The cause of this tragedy was never established,

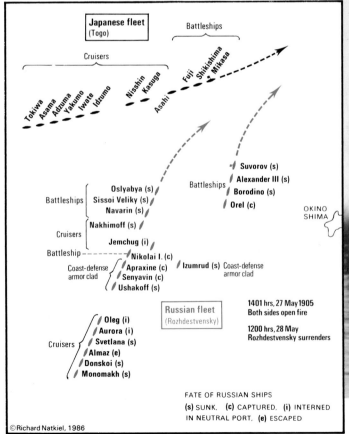

but suspicions remain to this day in Japan that it was an indication of the extent of disapproval of the peace terms.

If there was discontent in Japan, worse had taken place in Russia. The eruption of the 1905 Revolution was triggered by rising disgust at the conduct of the war, the Tsushima Straits being seen as the final straw.

As for the world at large, Tsushima had been the first major naval battle to take place since 1827, when the combined fleets of Britain, France and Russia decisively defeated the Turkish and Egyptian navies at Cape Navarino during the Greek War of Independence. Consequently it was subjected to much analysis and led to the rise of the Dreadnought, which was to be the basis of the naval race of the next ten years among the major powers.

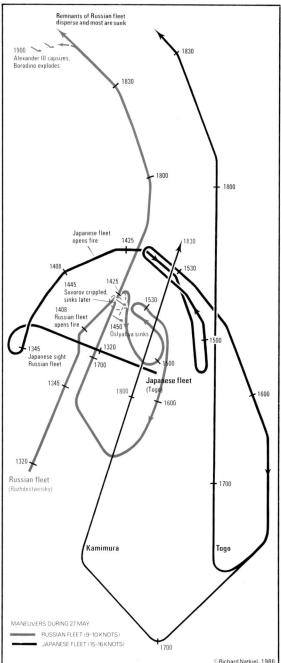

Remnants of Russian fleet disperse and most are sunk

1900
Alexander III capsizes, Borodino explodes

1830

1830

1800

1800

Japanese fleet opens fire

1425

1408

1445
Suvorov crippled, sinks later

1425

1530

1530

1408
Russian fleet opens fire

1450
Oslyabya sinks

1500

1345
Japanese sight Russian fleet

1320

1700

1500

1345

1800

Japanese fleet (Togo)

1600

1600

1320

1700

Russian fleet (Rozhdestvensky)

Kamimura

Togo

1700

MANEUVERS DURING 27 MAY
— RUSSIAN FLEET (9-10 KNOTS)
— JAPANESE FLEET (15-16 KNOTS)

© Richard Natkiel, 1986

TANNENBERG
1914

One of the most impressive victories achieved by the German Army in its history was that against the Russians at Tannenberg in 1914. So highly regarded was it that a memorial to the battle was erected in East Prussia after the war and a special ceremony was held there on its anniversary.

Tannenberg was born of the dilemma that dogged Germany's strategy on land, that of the danger of simultaneous war on two fronts. It was this problem which Count Alfred von Schlieffen had to first resolve when he was drawing up the master plan for the next war while he was Chief of Staff in the 1890s. What had triggered the necessity for this was the military alliance between France and Russia, which was formed in 1892. Should both combine against Germany, von Schlieffen concluded, France was bound to mobilize very much more quickly than her ally. Therefore she must be defeated first, while the German forces in the East remained on the defensive.

Planning for the East was very much dominated by the Polish salient, which, with Warsaw at its base, jutted towards Germany. To the north of it lay East Prussia and to the south the virtually impassable Pripet Marshes. Von Schlieffen's concept assumed that any Russian invasion of Germany would be mounted from the salient, but this presented the opportunity of inflicting a Cannae-type of defeat through

double-envelopment on the Russians. This would be achieved by simultaneous thrusts southeast from East Prussia and by the Austrians northeast round the Pripet Marshes from the south. The German forces detailed to carry out the attack from East Prussia would be deployed from the west once France was defeated, with just weak forces holding the Polish – German borders in the meantime.

The Russians were, at least in some ways, fortunate to have a war minister from 1909 who was determined to make good the weaknesses which

Previous pages: *German infantry during the opening days of the campaign in East Prussia.*

Above: *A German telegraph detachment preparing its midday meal.*

Below: *The Grand Duke Nicholas (left), the Russian commander, with Czar Nicholas II.*

Above: *Paul von Hindenburg, who was recalled from retirement to win the victory of Tannenberg. Later he became overall commander of the German armies and ended his life as President of Germany.*

Right: *General Rennekampf failed to capitalize on his initial success against the Germans, partially because he had not been able to complete his mobilization before being ordered to advance.*

Far left: *The deployment of the armies during the early stages of Tannenberg.*

had been so starkly revealed during the Russo-Japanese War. General Sukhomlinov worked hard to improve the spirit of technical and scientific progress within the armed forces. He also attempted to overhaul the inefficient and cumbersome resupply and reinforcement systems. Above all, he sought to close the existing three weeks' gap between the German and Russian mobilizations. One of the major measures that he took in this respect was to improve the railway system in western Russia, something that did not go unnoticed by the Germans. Von Moltke the Younger, now German Chief of Staff and nephew of the architect of victory over the French in 1870, decided in 1913 to amend the Schlieffen Plan in order to take into account the more speedy Russian mobilization. Consequently he decided to strengthen the East at the expense of the West, creating the Eighth Army of 210,000 men and 600 guns in order to provide a more effective defense. Appointed to command it was General von Prittwitz, whose corpulence provoked the nickname *der dicke Soldat* (the Fat Soldier).

The Russian plans were drawn up in consultation with the French, the final version being promulgated in 1913. While they were primarily concerned with Austro-Hungary, the Russians did concede to the French request that they pose sufficient threat to East Prussia to prevent the Germans from achieving immediate overwhelming numerical superiority in the West. Consequently, they formed two army groups. One was to take care of the Austrians, while the other, the North-West Group under General Jilinski would operate against East Prussia. Initially it would consist of two armies, Rennenkampf's First and Samsonov's Second, but they would be reinforced by a third army after the first month, when mobilization would be complete. Even so, the two armies still had a strength of 450,000 men, which gave them a superiority of over 2:1. The task of the First and Second Armies was to destroy the German Eighth Army and the plan to achieve this was much influenced by geographic factors. Stretching some 50 miles along the East Prussian north-south border with Russia were the Masurian Lakes, which provided an effective defensive obstacle. Therefore Jilinski decided that Rennenkampf should operate to the north of the Lakes, while Samsonov attacked northwards from Poland and to their west, the idea being to destroy the German army between the Lakes and the River Vistula.

On 17 August 1914, 16 days after Germany's declaration of war on Russia, while the German armies in the West were overrunning Belgium and the French offensive into Lorraine was being brought to a bloody halt, the Russian armies began their advance. At the same time

the Austro-Hungarian forces struck towards Lublin as the southern prong of the Schlieffen 'Cannae' plan, and the Russian South-West Group began a major thrust through Galicia. In the north, Rennenkampf, having brushed aside von Prittwitz's outposts at Stallupönen, came up against the German main body at Gumbinnen, and a battle was fought here on the 20th. German I Corps, commanded by von Francois, who was to gain the nickname of 'the Fox' on account of his ability to turn up in unexpected places, drove back the Russian right wing some seven miles. In the center, however, matters did not go so well. Von Mackensen's XVII Corps made a crude frontal attack, was repulsed, and his troops began to display signs of panic. This forced von Francois to withdraw as well. Consequently, what could have been a German victory turned out to be a Russian one, but Rennenkampf, instead of closely following up his success, halted to savor the fruits of it. Samsonov, believing that Rennenkampf had won a decisive victory, now began his thrust into East Prussia without informing his fellow army commander. The fact that the two did not get on with one another and are reputed to have come to blows on Mukden railway station in 1905 may have had something to do with this.

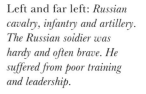

Left and far left: *Russian cavalry, infantry and artillery. The Russian soldier was hardy and often brave. He suffered from poor training and leadership.*

Bottom: *General Samsonov. His rash thrust into East Prussia from the south played into von Hindenburg's and Ludendorff's hands.*

The reverse at Gumbinnen was sufficient to panic von Prittwitz, now aware of the threat from Samsonov to his right flank, to wish to pull back across the Vistula. His corps commanders were admantly against this, especially because of Rennenkampf's failure to keep contact with their withdrawing forces, but von Prittwitz over-rode them and informed von Moltke by telephone of his intention. Von Prittwitz's staff now managed to persuade him to change his mind. Instead of withdrawing across the Vistula, he would strike at Samsonov's left wing, and orders for this were given out on the evening of the 20th. There was a major risk in this, in that it was dependent on Rennenkampf remaining where he was. Only in these circumstances could forces be transferred to attack Samsonov. Von Prittwitz's change of heart came, however, too late to save him, especially since he failed to tell von Moltke what he was now doing.

Von Moltke had already decided that the Eighth Army commander was a liability. On 22 August a telegram was sent to 67 year-old General Paul von Hindenburg, now living in retirement at Hanover, asking if he would take von Prittwitz's place. His reply was: 'I am

ready.' At the same time von Moltke appointed General Erich von Ludendorff to be von Hindenburg's Chief of Staff. He himself was commanding an infantry brigade in Belgium at the time and, on hearing the news, immediately motored to von Moltke's headquarters at Koblenz. Here he was instructed to concentrate on destroying Samsonov, stripping fortresses of their troops in order to build up a sufficient force, and orders were sent to von Prittwitz to this effect. Von Ludendorff then motored to Hannover, collected von Hindenburg, and the two arrived at Marienburg in East Prussia on the 23rd.

To their surprise, von Hindenburg and von Ludendorff found that von Prittwitz's staff had already set in train the plan that had been formulated at Koblenz. Indeed, this shows how the German General Staff was so trained as to be able to think as one. Rennenkampf's army had still made no further forward moves and Samsonov had driven back part of XX Corps. More significant was the intelligence on Russian intentions. Samsonov's plan was known from a Russian wireless message which had been sent uncoded, while Jilinski's overall plan for the First and Second Armies had been found on a captured Russian officer. Security was not a Russian strength.

Samsonov himself was advancing on a 60 mile front and very much further to the west than Jilinski had laid down. This was in the belief that he could swing his left round behind the Germans, but moving on such a wide axis inevitably caused gaps, something which the Germans were quick to note. Rennenkampf, too, began to move forward, but only slowly. Hence von Hindenburg and von Ludendorff now took an even greater risk. They reduced the troops in front of the Russian First Army to merely two cavalry brigades. It took, as von Ludendorff later wrote, 'strong nerves' to do this, but it was seen as crucial if the German plan to take advantage of the increasing gaps in Samsonov's front was to work.

On 26 August the attack on the Russian Second Army was launched. While half of XX Corps, supported by Landwehr (local defense forces) held Samsonov in the center, von Francois's corps, together with the remainder of XX Corps, struck the Russian left at Usdau and I Reserve and XVII Corps attacked the Russian

Above: *The entrapment of the Russian Second Army. Although a seeming risk to leave little more than a cavalry screen in front of the Russian First Army, the Germans were confident, partly thanks to wireless intercepts, that its advance would be only hesitant, thus enabling them to concentrate on destroying Samsonov's army.*

Left: *German machine gun posts once the fighting in East Prussia had died down in the autumn.*

Above left: *Always an encouraging sight for troops moving towards the battle. Prussian Guards pass Russian prisoners, the first of many, being escorted back from Tannenberg.*

Below left: *German defenses overlooking the Masurian Lakes.*

right. Samsonov, with no clear picture of what was happening, dashed across to see his extreme left hand corps, with little understanding of the threat that was developing on his right. This, however, did not prevent panic and confusion and on the following day this wing began to come apart. In the meantime, while the Russian center continued to push forward, the right wing was also in trouble. The two German corps had succeeded in isolating the Russian VI Corps and sent it flying pell mell southwards. Thus, by the end of the second day both Russian wings had been virtually broken, although they were making progress in the center against the portion of XX Corps. North of the Masurian Lakes, on the other hand, Rennenkampf continued to plod forwards seemingly unaware of the crisis developing to the south.

Yet, such is often the fog of war, the Germans were not totally aware of the predicament that Samsonov was now in. Indeed, on the night 27/28 August, von Ludendorff, worried over the Russian progress in the center, ordered von Francois to bring his corps round to the north in order to stiffen XX Corps. He, however, ignored this, for he had seen an opportunity to entirely cut Samsonov off from his base. Thus he had already begun to swing round to the south of the Russian left wing and was now racing eastwards. Von Ludendorff, his equilibrium restored, also realized that von Francois's advance could enable the Russian center to be trapped. He therefore ordered I Reserve and XVII Corps, who had been engaging the Russian VI Corps on the right, to leave it to its own devices and advance south to Willenberg in order to join hands with von Francois. The German center would also switch to the offensive. Thus Samsonov was to be squeezed from all directions. On the 28th, while von Francois blocked the rear of the Russian center in the Niedenburg area, the German center, after meeting significant resistance during the morning, began to drive the Russian corps back. The German VII Corps on the extreme right made rapid progress from the start.

By now Samsonov had lost what little grip he had on the battle. Worse, his resupply system was in tatters, largely because of the wide frontage on which he had originally advanced. Even so, on 29 August, the Russians did provoke one final crisis. Their I Corps, on the extreme left, which had escaped von Francois's enveloping move by withdrawing to the southeast, now came back into the fray and attacked the rear of the German I Corps. What hopes the Russians had of forcing the German grip to weaken were dashed by the end of the day, however, as the Russian I Corps was sent reeling back. Next day, 30 August, the Russian center was totally surrounded, with only the remnants of I and VI

Corps on the extreme flanks being able to escape.

'A day of harvesting,' von Ludendorff termed 31 August. By the end of it the Germans had 92,000 prisoners in their hands, including two corps commanders. A further estimated 70,000 Russians lay dead and almost all the Second Army's guns also fell into German hands. The total German casualties were 15,000 killed, wounded and missing. As for Samsonov, he set off on foot, accompanied by five staff officers, through the forests and made for the Russian frontier. After a time he fell behind the others and was not seen again. It is believed that he shot himself.

Tannenberg was a disaster of epic proportions for Russian arms and its symbolism for Germans arms came to mean more than just turning back the Russian invasion. Von Hindenburg selected the title of the battle from a village of that name which lies between Usdau and Hohenstein. He did so, not because it had played any major part, but on account of the fact that it had been here in July 1410 that the seemingly invincible Teutonic Knights had been decisively defeated by the Poles, Bohemians, Lithuanians and Russians. Now, 500 years later, he felt that the reverse had been aptly avenged.

Yet, disaster as it was for the Russians, Tannenberg had only destroyed one of their eight

Below: *Bewildered Russians surrender.*

armies then in the field. Six were enjoying a measure of success against the Austrians, and Rennenkampf's First Army still occupied a significant area of East Prussia. It was to this that von Hindenburg's attention now turned. With Rennenkampf's southern wing anchored on the Masurian Lakes, von Hindenburg planned to outflank him in the north, close to the Baltic, and bring about his destruction in that way. He therefore deployed his troops accordingly, but the Russians, sensing what was happening began to withdraw on 9 September and, on the following day, even counter-attacked to give themselves more time. Although they lost another 60,000 men, they were able to extricate themselves and, on the 13th, withdraw across the River Niemen to fight another day.

Simultaneously, in the West the Battle of the Marne was being fought. It would result in the final demise of the Schlieffen Plan as the German armies were first halted east of Paris and then forced to withdraw. They themselves believed that one reason for this failure was that during their advance von Moltke had switched nine divisions from the vital right wing of the great wheel to the Eastern Front in spite of von Ludendorff's protestations that this was unnecessary. Von Moltke himself later admitted that this was a mistake and that with them he could both have encompassed Paris and outflanked the Allied left. Thus, the Russian

advance into East Prussia could have been said to have fulfilled its object in denying the Germans their quick victory in the West and that Tannenberg was a worthwhile price to pay for this. Certainly, the Germans were forced to change their strategy by going on to the defensive in the West and Tannenberg did not prevent the Russian war machine from resisting the Central Powers for three more years. When it was finally destroyed, it was from within, through the forces of revolution, rather than without.

Above: *Russian prisoners of war.*

Left: *The dead of Tannenberg.*

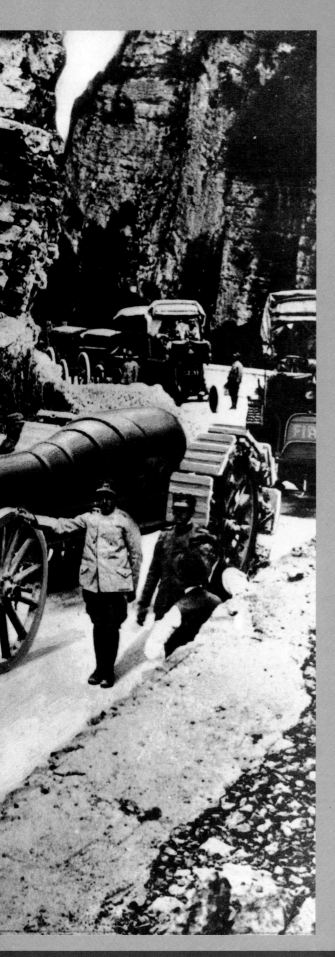

CAPORETTO
1917

Previous pages: *Italian heavy artillery being moved up to the Isonzo front. That of the Austrians was more modern and in greater numbers.*

Above left: *A German supply column during the preparation phase of the Austro-German attack.*

Above right: *German stormtroops crossing the Isonzo in pursuit of the withdrawing Italians.*

Below: *Italian officers testing gasmasks. Even with this protection the use of gas shells during the opening barrage did much to disrupt the Italian defenses.*

Military disasters can often be caused by the fact that the armies which suffer them have low morale and hence will break more easily. Morale itself can be drastically influenced, not just by factors such as poor leadership and lack of food, ammunition, and other supplies, but also because the conflict in which they are involved does not enjoy popular support at home. Such was the case with Italy during the years 1915-17.

Italy had originally been a member of the Triple Alliance formed in 1882 with Germany and Austro-Hungary. She had, however, continued to maintain friendly relations with Britain, France and Russia. Furthermore, her relations with Austria had gradually worsened because of rivalry in the Balkans and also because Austria continued to hold the region at the head of the Adriatic, including Trieste, territory which the Italians considered belonged to them. In any event, Austria did not consult her in July 1914 over going to war, and Italy still had 50,000 troops tied up in Libya, which she had recently wrested from the Turks. It was thus hardly surprising that when war did break out Italy declared her neutrality. Some more nationalist elements, among whom was a young newspaper editor, Benito Mussolini, believed that it was wrong to stay out of the war arguing that it would detract from Italy's stand-ing as a major power. They were, however, a minority.

Nevertheless, the Italian government was prepared to make overtures to both sides in the hope of being granted territorial concessions as the price for declaring war. Both, too, were keen for Italy to join them, especially because of her geostrategic position. Austria, strongly backed by Germany, entered into detailed negotiations with the Italians during the early months of 1915. There with discussions, too, with London, Paris, and the Russians. In the end it was the Allied expedition to the Dardanelles, which was launched in March 1915, that tipped the

balance. At the end of April a secret treaty was signed by which Italy agreed to enter the war in return for a promise that at the victorious end of it she would be granted the territory that she had long desired at the head of the Adriatic, as well as the Dodecanese. Thus on 23 May 1915 Italy declared war on Austria, but would not do so against Germany until August the following year.

The war on which Italy embarked was to be fought on a front of 350 miles, stretching from the border with Switzerland to the River Isonzo

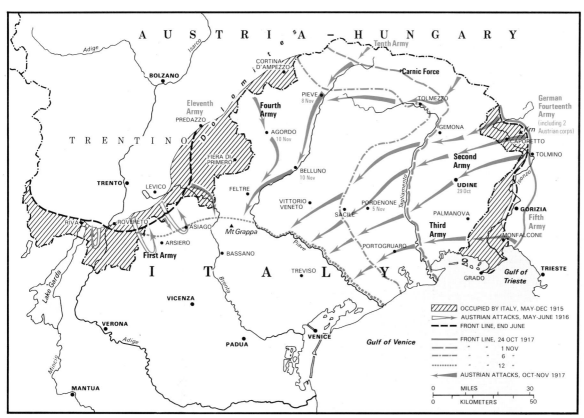

Above: *General Luigi Cadorna, the Italian commander-in-chief from Italy's entry into the war, who conducted the many battles on the Isonzo and Trentino fronts.*

Left: *Compared with previous battles on the Italian Front, Caporetto represented a major disaster and Cadorna's removal from command was inevitable.*

at the head of the Adriatic. Only in the extreme east, in the Isonzo River valley, was the arena not mountainous. Since the mountains held overwhelming advantages for the defense, the Isonzo was the only area in which the Italians could attack with any chance of success. Consequently, from June 1915, they were to launch repeated assaults here. Between summer 1915 and summer 1917 there would be 11 battles of the Isonzo. They gained little ground, but cost the Italians over one million casualties.

Throughout the first two years of the war the Italian government did little to stiffen its people's resolve. There was little censorship and the Socialists, who had not supported entry into the war, became increasingly vehement in their denunciation of it. Their press viewed the conflict as a class struggle, and the mounting casualties served to fuel their propaganda. Aided and abetted by the Communists, their slogan during summer 1917 became 'Next winter not another man in the trenches'. In the light of all this it is not surprising that morale within the Italian Army deteriorated.

Yet, General Luigi Cadorna, the Italian Chief of Staff, was determined to keep attacking and managed in September 1917 to persuade the British and French to send him 200 heavy guns, something he was desperately short of, in order to support his attacks. No sooner were these guns on their way from France than Cadorna changed his mind. He decided that the Austrians and Germans were preparing to launch an offensive and told the British and French that he must now remain on the defensive. Italy's allies considered that he had obtained the guns from them under false pretences and immediately ordered the bulk of them to return to the Western Front. This served to fill Cadorna with gloom.

He was, however, right in believing that an attack was being planned. The Austrians, who were also being bled white by the attrition battles, had continually pestered the Germans for reinforcements so that they could launch a decisive offensive. The Germans had been unwilling to draw off troops from other fronts, but at the beginning of September 1917, with the British making little progress in their offensive in the Ypres area, and the Russians crumbling after the failure of their 1917 offensive, they relented. A mountain warfare expert, General Krafft von Dellmensingen was sent to the Isonzo front to examine an attack plan which had first been put forward by the Austrians in 1916. This was to attack across the River Isonzo, using a small bridgehead held by the Austrians in the Tolmino area as the main jumping-off point, and drive the Italian Second and Third Armies back behind the Tagliamento, some 40 miles to the rear.

The main assault was to be carried out by the German Fourteenth Army under General Otto von Below. This consisted of nine German and seven Austrian divisions, together with *Jaeger* (light infantry) and storm battalions. Von Below's attack would be supported in the north by part of the Austrian Tenth Army, and in the south by the Austrian Second Isonzo and later the First Isonzo Armies. A large concentration of guns was built up – the Fourteenth Army had no less than 1845, of which 492 were German 240mm mortars. Furthermore, a significant amount of their ammunition was gas shells. The attack was originally scheduled for 20 October, but on the 10th heavy and continuous rain began to fall and this forced postponements.

Cadorna's early belief that an attack was being prepared was based on indicators purposely presented to him by the Austrians that it would come further west in the River Trentino area just to the north of Lake Garda. In early October, however, Italian reconnaissance had

Above: German mountain artillery passes through Vittorio-Veneto lying on a tributary of the River Livenza, 8 November 1917. The Allied offensive a year later, which gave Italy her revenge, would take its name from this town.

Above: *Italian 149mm gun. The difficulty of moving them meant that many were abandoned during the retreat to the Piave.*

Left: *Austrian machine gun post.*

Below: *German storm troops keep up the pressure.*

identified 43 Austrian and German divisions along the whole front. Of these 18 were opposite the Italian Second Army and 11½ in front of the Third Army. Furthermore, additional divisions were spotted approaching the Isonzo. The message was clear; the attack would be launched here, and soon. This was further confirmed by a number of soldiers who crossed into Italian lines in the days before the offensive began.

Cadorna did not sit idly by. He had, however, a problem with the commander of the Italian Second Army, which was to bear the brunt of the attack. General Capello's troops held the front between Flitsch in the north and Gorizia in the south. He himself believed that attack was the best form of defense and wanted to assault up the Vrh Valley and from the Bainsizza plateau south of Caporetto in order to take the enemy there in the left flank. He therefore had concentrated all his reserves here, leaving nothing to support the left wing of his sector. Cadorna countermanded this attack, but

Above: *Italian propaganda art – Alpini (mountain) troops attacking an Austrian trench.*

Opposite above: *It looks like artistic license, but this method of getting guns up mountains was often used on the Italian Front.*

Opposite below: *Signs of panic. Abandoned Italian transport on a road back to the Piave.*

Capello did nothing to adjust his reserves. In fact, he was sick in bed at this time, but refused to relinquish his command and allow himself to be taken to hospital. Too late, Cadorna realized that around Caporetto itself and to the north the line was held with just two battalions to the mile as opposed to eight elsewhere. He ordered a division to be deployed to this sector from the south, but it was still on the move when the storm broke.

At 2.00am on 24 October the Austro-German artillery opened fire on a front extending from the Adriatic northwards for some 60 miles. The sector around Caporetto itself, which was the *point d'appui* of the attack, was subjected also to two and a half hours of gas shells. Initially there was a spirited reply from the Italian artillery, but gradually its fire died away, as did the beams from the searchlights. The gas had begun to take its toll. There was then a pause for two and a half hours, before, at 7.00am, there was a crash of high explosive fire along the front. It was directed at headquarters, ammunition dumps, approach roads and artillery positions. This followed a technique which had been first used, with success, against the Russians at Riga at the beginning of the previous month and was designed to cause maximum disruption to the enemy's command and control. As the bombardment opened so the

attacking troops rose out of their trenches. Snow on the high ground and rain and mist below gave them cover.

So numbed were the defenders that there was little resistance in the Caporetto sector and the attackers were only forced to halt for a time to enable their artillery to be brought up. By 4.00pm the Austrians and Germans were across the Isonzo and Caporetto had fallen to them. In the south the defenses were in greater depth and progress was slower. Cadorna himself, in spite of the virtual breakdown of his command, control and communications, was soon aware of the ever more severe situation around Caporetto and tried desperately to get reinforcements from Tenth Army in the north and Third Army in the south moved across to Second Army in order to plug the gap. It was, however, hopeless. Matters were made worse by the low morale of the Italian troops. Panic began to grip some units and they started to leave their positions and retreat to the rear. By midnight Cadorna was beginning to fear for the worst and ordered General Capello, still at his post in spite of a severe attack of influenza, and the Duke of d'Aosta commanding the Third Army to begin discreetly preparing a new defense line along the Tagliamento.

On the second day of the battle the situation deteriorated further. Cadorna ordered the Duke d'Aosta to withdraw his medium and heavy artillery not just behind the Talgiamento, but to the River Piave, a further 30 miles to the rear. The sick Capello also came and requested permission to immediately pull back to the Tagliamento. Cadorna agreed to this, but Capello, while working on the orders for the withdrawal, collapsed. General Montouri, who took over from him, had little idea of the true situation and consulted with his corps commanders. For some reason, presumably because they were also out of touch with their troops, they argued that it was better to hold in their present positions. As they did so, troops were fleeing in panic towards the Tagliamento. Yet, some Italian units, especially the crack Alpini did continue to cling to their positions in the mountains until their ammunition ran out. It was in battles with these that a young German officer, commanding a company of mountain troops, won Prussia's highest decoration, the *Pour Le Mérite*, for his capture of Mounts Mzrli and Matajur. His name was Erwin Rommel, and 25 years later he was to be a household name, not only in Germany but elsewhere as well.

During the next two days matters went from bad to worse. On the 27th Cadorna finally ordered a withdrawal behind the Tagliamento; this was to apply to the Tenth Army in the north as well. The Italian Third Army, which still remained largely intact, began in good order, but confusion quickly set in as the withdrawal routes became clogged, a problem magnified by a mass of civilian refugees. The Second Army, which was in a much more chaotic state at the outset, was supposed to hold the line of the River Torre until the 29th to enable the Third Army to get clear, but pressure on it and increasing panic meant that the Germans were already across the river by the early hours of that day and driving hard for Cadorna's own headquarters at Udine. By this time Second Army had been split into two and was disintegrating. Yet, the Austro-German advance was beginning to slow. The troops were becoming very tired, there was a tendency to fall off the line of march in order to forage for food, and they had also been surprised at the suddenness of the Italian collapse. Nevertheless, on the evening of the 29th, von Below ordered the seizure of the bridges over the Tagliamento before they could be destroyed. This was, of course, going beyond the original plan, which called merely for an advance to the river. At much the same time, Ludendorff, now Chief of Staff on the Western Front, asked when he could have his divisions back. Von Below's reply was that they would be returned once the Tagliamento had been crossed. The Austrian Chief of Staff, von Arz, however, was now looking to more ambitious objectives, and told the

Left: *More signs of an army in hasty retreat.*

Below: *Austrian troops in the pursuit. Eventually the rate of advance required to prevent the Italians from regrouping on the Piave proved too much for the attackers.*

Germans that no troops should be withdrawn until the Piave was reached. Even so, the dash to the Tagliamento did not go as planned. Subordinate commanders took matters into their own hands in their efforts to annihilate the Italian armies. The result was that they cut across each other's axes of advance which led to confusion. Consequently, Cadorna was able to get back and establish himself on the Tagliamento, although his troops had been forced to abandon much of their heavy equipment and some 60,000 had been made prisoner.

During 31 October and on the following two days the Italians successfully held off frontal assaults made across the river against them and it seemed as though the situation could be stabilized. Indeed, Cadorna, who had a few days earlier asked for 20 British and French divisions to be sent immediately to bail him out, now told them that these were not all needed and that he was happy to accept the six which they had already begun to send him. On the night of 2/3 November the situation suddenly changed. An Austrian division and a German one succeeded in getting across the river well to the north, between Cornino and Pinzano. This was too much for the Italian Second Army, on top of the punishment it had already received, and it broke and ran. On the afternoon of the 3rd Cadorna was forced to tell his government that the Tagliamento Line had collapsed and to ask permission to withdraw behind the Piave. At the same time the British and French were asked to send 15 divisions to establish a new line here. Eventually the the British and French agreed to send two British and six French divisions, but by this time they had become so irritated by Cadorna's continual changes of mind that they demanded his removal. On 9 November, after having just issued an Order of the Day exhorting his soldiers to 'die and not to yield' on the Piave, Cadorna was informed of his dismis-

Left: *Another shot of Germans crossing the Isonzo under desultory Italian artillery fire.*

Below left: *Austrian troops round up Italian prisoners.*

Below: *Some of the Italians who perished during the battle.*

sal. By now his troops were back behind the river, while the Austro-German advance had run out of steam. On 16 November they launched attacks on the Piave, but these were easily repulsed, the defenders now stiffened by newly arrived French and British troops.

The disaster at Caporetto cost the Italians over 300,000 casualties. Significantly, though, 85 percent of these were prisoners of war, an indication of how morale had crumbled. In addition, the Central Powers captured over 3,000 guns and vast quantities of stores. Yet, rather than leading to the wholesale collapse of Italy the opposite was the case. Led by King Victor Emmanuel, who declared that soldiers and civilians must be a 'single army' and that 'all cowardice is treachery, all discord is treachery, all recrimination is treachery', the Italian people became united for the first time in the war. A year later the Italian Army was to have its revenge when, at the Battle of Vittorio-Veneto, it drove the Austrians back across the Isonzo and into Austria itself.

THE FALL OF FRANCE
1940

The German Blitzkrieg which struck France and the Low Countries in 1940 was a demonstration of what happens when one side is caught wrong-footed at the start of a campaign and is prevented by sheer pace from recovering and wresting the initiative from the attacker. It also showed how much war had changed now that the internal combustion engine had come of age.

When France and Britain went to war in 1939 they were from the outset, unwilling to launch a major attack into Germany in order to relieve pressure on the Poles. True, the French did make a limited foray into the Saarland, but they were reluctant to advance outside the range of the guns in the Maginot Line, which had become the bulwark of their defense. The British, who had to transport their army across the English Channel (the first elements did not land in France until 9 September), were in no position to mount an immediate offensive. Consequently the Poles were left to cope on their own and their fate was sealed when the Russians (in alliance with Germany) invaded on 17 September.

The Western Allies believed that if Hitler attacked them he would probably attempt a repeat of 1914, with the German armies sweeping through Belgium and then wheeling south and east through northern France in order to cut the French and British off from the Channel before enveloping them. Indeed, this was the basis of the original German Plan Yellow for the strike westwards. Consequently, during autumn 1939 much effort was made to extend the Maginot Line by fortifying the Franco-Belgian frontier. The main problem was that in northeastern France there was no obvious natural obstacle upon which to base a defense, unless the Allies were prepared to sacrifice a goodly portion of French territory, which, for understandable reasons, they were not.

In November 1939, however, after much discussion, the French and British completed a new defense plan, known as Plan D. Belgium offered a number of convenient waterways – the Albert Canal, and the Rivers Dyle and Meuse which could be used at the center of a strategic defense. To fight the battle on one of these was attractive, especially since it would markedly reduce the collateral damage done to French industry, much of which was in the vulnerable northeast. Therefore, once the Germans crossed the frontiers the left wing of the Allied forces – the French First and Seventh Armies and the British Expeditionary Force (BEF) – would advance into Belgium and take up positions along these waterways. There were two snags to this. Firstly, Belgium was determined to maintain her neutrality and would not allow

Previous pages: *German artillery parades in the Bois de Boulogne, Paris, June 1940, and the Junkers Ju 87 Stuka divebomber, a psychological as well as physical weapon system.*

even reconnaissance parties across its borders. Also, the Allies committed their best armies to the move forward into Belgium, the French First and Seventh Armies and the BEF.

Hitler himself was impatient to attack the Western Allies as soon as possible after the successful conclusion to the Polish campaign. Indeed, his original target date was as early as 12 November 1939. His generals were not happy about this. Several lessons from Poland needed to be assimilated; more time was needed both to deploy and train the troops, and to assemble the necessary materiel. Furthermore, the seasonal fogs would hinder air support. The aim that Hitler had laid down was to defeat as large a portion of the Allied forces as possible and seize sufficient territory in the Low Countries in order to wage successful maritime and air operations against Britain. Three army groups would be involved. Fedor von Bock's Army Group B was to take the leading role, overrun-

Top: *The Phony War. British troops recreate the 1914-18 trench atmosphere.*

Above: *British prime minister Neville Chamberlain with his 'scrap of paper' brought back from Munich in 1938. He misread Hitler again in spring 1940 when he stated that the Germans had missed the chance of attacking in the West.*

Above: *Somewhere in Belgium, May 1940. German troops have used their ingenuity to overcome this demolished bridge.*

Above right: *General Heinz Guderian, the main inspiration behind the German Blitzkrieg tactics. He more than lived up to his nickname,* Schnelle Heinz *(Fast Heinz) in May 1940.*

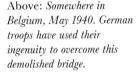

ning Holland and Belgium and then the extreme northeast of France. Gerd von Rundstedt's Army Group A would advance on von Bock's southern flank, conforming to his movements. Finally, Ritter von Leeb's Army Group C would mask the Maginot Line. Von Rundstedt and his chief of staff, Erich von Manstein, besides objecting to Hitler's impatience to put Plan Yellow into practice, also viewed it as flawed in its aim, which was far too limited and could only achieve a partial victory. Instead, the objective should be the total defeat of the Allied forces. Furthermore, to give von Bock the decisive role made no sense since the Belgian fortifications and waterways favored the defense, which von Bock would be tackling head on. Rather, Army Group A should play the decisive part by launching a thrust through the wooded Ardennes and cutting off the Allied forces in Belgium and northeast France.

Von Rundstedt's and von Manstein's propo-

sal initially fell on deaf ears. Indeed, it did not get beyond Walther von Brauchitsch, the German Army Commander in Chief, whose energies continued to be directed at persuading Hitler to delay the attack. As it happened, it was the weather, rather than military arguments , which had the final say. Nevertheless, von Rundstedt and his chief of staff continued to press their case. They were reinforced in this by the deployment of XIX Panzer Corps to Army Group A, which originally had been allocated no armor. This was commanded by General Heinz Guderian, the driving force behind the German Panzer arm. This was as well, since in February 1940, von Manstein was removed from his position as Chief of Staff Army Group A and given command of an infantry corps, partly perhaps, as a means of shutting him up. In the meantime, Hitler had ordered the attack to be launched at first light on 17 January, but a week before this a Luftwaffe aircraft, having lost its way in fog, crashed at Mechelen in Belgium. On board was a staff officer carrying the plans for Case Yellow. He tried to burn them, but was only partially successful and the charred remnants fell into Belgian hands. Since it was now likely that the plan had been compromised, a further postponement was ordered. Then bad weather struck once more (the winter 1939-40 in Western Europe turned out to be one of the coldest on record) and Hitler decided to set no more attack dates in advance, but merely to keep his forces at 24 hour readiness. Towards the end of February, he finally came round to Army Group A's way of thinking, and a revised plan was issued calling for the main thrust to be made by von Rundstedt through the Ardennes.

This period of waiting, termed the *Sitzkrieg* by

Right: *Erich von Manstein, architect of the revised Plan Yellow for the overrunning of the West.*

Below: *The opening moves in May 1940. The deployment of the northern Allied armies into Belgium played into the German hands.*

the Germans and the 'Phony War' by an American journalist, should have been to the Allies' benefit. Certainly, it enabled the BEF to be enlarged, but many of the divisions sent across were poorly equipped. It also did little for the morale of the French troops. They were not given enough to do with boredom creating discontent and absenteeism. Matters were not helped by a very cumbersome command structure. The overall commander, Marshal Maurice Gamelin, had merely a civil telephone connecting him to his principal subordinate, General Joseph Georges, who was titled Commander-in-Chief North-East. He, in turn, had three army groups under command, under which came the various armies including the BEF. On the air side, the command and control organization merely served to confuse. While the Allied air forces were nominally under command of the chief of the French Air Force, General Vuillemin, they were also organized into zones of air operations, which equated to the army sectors. These were controlled by another General and consequently air units often received two sets of conflicting orders. Another Allied weakness was in the way that the armor was deployed. They had numerical superiority over the Germans in terms of numbers of tanks – some 3500 as against 2570 – but while the Germans had theirs concentrated in Panzer divisions, the Allies dispersed their tanks. True, both the British and French had formed armored divisions, but the British 1st Armoured Division was still seriously lacking in equipment and would not be sent to France until towards the end of May. As for the French, they had four armored divisions on paper, but the first two of these were not formed until January 1940, and the fourth, under Colonel Charles de Gaulle, would not come into being until May.

With the coming of spring the likelihood of a German attack increased, but Hitler's attention was diverted by Scandinavia and his wish to forestall Allied designs on Norway. On 9 April the Germans invaded Denmark and Norway, overrunning the former in one day. Anglo-French forces were sent to Norway, but their employment had been too hurriedly thought out and they were unable to prevent the Germans from securing the whole country in a campaign that lasted just two months. In the meantime, there was a belief that the Germans had delayed too long in the West and that the Allies were now too strong for them. British Prime Minister Neville Chamberlain crowed on 5 April that Hitler had 'missed the bus'. Five weeks later he would be forced to eat his words.

On 30 April 1940 Hitler warned his armies in the West to be prepared to launch their attacks any time after 5 May. On the night 9/10 May the codeword 'Danzig' was issued and at 3.00am the

Above: *German Panzers on the march. Their high speed advance paralysed the Allied higher command.*

Above right: *Ju 87 Stukas. They proved, as they had done so in Poland, to be a most effective form of aerial artillery.*

following morning Luftwaffe aircraft took off to attack Allied airfields. Two hours later the German armies crossed the borders of Holland, Belgium and Luxembourg, while airborne and airlanded troops seized key points in Holland and what had been believed to be the impregnable fortress of Eben Emael in Belgium. Nevertheless, the Allies remained steadfast to Plan D and Billotte's First Army Group crossed the Belgian border in order to take up its predesignated positions on the Belgian waterways.

The Netherlands and northern Belgium were speedily overrun, with the Dutch surrendering on 15 May, the day after Rotterdam had been largely devastated in an attack by the Luftwaffe. Meanwhile, von Rundstedt's armor had wound its way through the hilly and wooded Ardennes and on 12 May reached the Meuse. The three Panzer groups into which it was organized now prepared to cross at Dinant (General Hoth), Monthermé (Reinhardt) and Sedan (Guderian). Because the Allies had not expected the Germans to attack from this direction their troops holding the line of the Meuse were not of good quality. During the 13th they were subjected to heavy artillery fire and also attacks by the Luftwaffe, especially the Ju 87 Stuka dive-

bomber, which was fitted with a siren in order to increase its terror effect. By nightfall all three Panzer groups had established small bridgeheads across the river. That night pontoon bridges were constructed and the tanks began to pass across. The Allies now began to become aware of the developing threat. Aircraft were sent to bomb the bridges over the Meuse, but in spite of displaying much courage, they failed to make an impression and suffered heavy casualties (over half the RAF's strength of 63 Fairey Battle fighter-bombers was lost in the first five days of the campaign, most in the attacks on the Meuse bridges). The French XXI Corps, of one armored, one mechanized and one cavalry divisions, was ordered to strike Guderian in the flank and drive him back across the Meuse, but the passage of orders was too slow for it to be able to react in time. Consequently, by dawn on 15 May Guderian had sufficient strength within his bridgehead to be confident of mounting a successful breakout, and at the end of the day he, Hoth and Reinhardt were racing westwards.

On 16 May it became clear to the Allies that the Panzer thrust was in danger of cutting off their armies in Belgium. Consequently orders were given to them to begin to withdraw. Those units in 1st Army Group who had made contact with von Bock's men found it difficult to accept this order since they considered that they had given a good account of themselves and were confident of being able to hold the Germans. Nevertheless, it was an order that had to be obeyed and the withdrawal began. Yet, the Germans, too, were displaying signs of nervousness. The deeper the Panzer swathe was cut westwards the longer its exposed southern flank became. True, there was a motorized infantry corps following in the path of the armor, but the bulk of the infantry was reliant on its feet and it was this that was supposed to guard the left flank. Von Rundstedt himself was convinced that the Allies would mount a counterstroke from the south. As we have seen, the French had tried to do so on the 14th. The upshot was that, having spoken to von Rundstedt, Ewald von Kleist, who was commanding the three Panzer groups, ordered them to halt at dusk on the 16th in order to allow the infantry to catch up. Guderian, believing that this would merely give the Allies a valuable breathing-space, was

furious and threatened to resign his command. Von Rundstedt had to intervene personally and smooth Guderian's ruffled feathers by permitting him to conduct reconnaissance in force, which to Guderian meant that he could continue his thrust. Nevertheless, Hitler himself was also nervous and visited von Rundstedt that same day, the 16th, in order to reassure himself that Army Group A was paying sufficient attention to its flanks.

On the following day the French did make another attempt to strike at the southern flank. De Gaulle's newly formed 4th Armored Divi-

Left: *Elements of the British 50th Northumbrian Division, and a Bren Gun Carrier* (below left) *during the Allied advance to the River Dyle.*

Below: *An abandoned French Char B2 heavy tank.*

Left: *German paratroopers dropping from Ju 52 transports over Holland, 10 May 1940.*

Below: *German motorcycle troops. The Panzer Division reconnaissance battalion had a company of these.*

Above left: *German paratroops landing on Dutch soil. Holland's neutrality made her ill-prepared for the German onslaught.*

Above: *German paratroops linking up with infantry on the outskirts of Rotterdam.*

Left: *Elements of the British 1st Armoured Division, which only landed at Cherbourg on 23 May, when the issue in north-eastern France was virtually decided.*

Below: *The ruins of a French town that had succumbed to overwhelming German firepower.*

Right: *A German artillery crew bombards a small chateau.*

sion struck Guderian's flank screen in the afternoon and entered Montcornet, cutting the 1st Panzer Division's supply lines. The French tanks, however, lacked infantry and artillery support and, also running short of fuel, were soon forced to withdraw, harried by the Luftwaffe as they did so. The Germans considered this blow of such little significance that von Kleist did not bother to pass the news of it upwards, and the following morning the Panzer spearheads entered St Quentin and Cambrai by mid-morning on the 17th. Aware of the French 1st Army Group's withdrawal from Belgium, Hoth's Panzer corps was now directed on Arras in order to cut it off, while Reinhardt and Guderian were to continue on a wider sweep in order to take them to the Channel.

Gamelin had finally realized that the only way that the German thrust could be defeated would be to cut it off at the shoulders by simultaneous attacks against its neck. He gave orders to this efect before being dismissed and replaced by Maxime Weygand on 19 May. To this end, Lord Gort, commanding the BEF received orders from London to move south from Amiens and attack any German forces encountered. With German tanks reported in Amiens on the 20th, however, Gort became concerned over his lines of communication with the Channel, and was loathe to commit a large force. Yet, he did recognize the threat to Arras, which was now being approached by Rommel's 7th Panzer

Division. Gort therefore mounted an attack on the 21st in order to knock Rommel off balance. This was carried out by 1st Army Tank Brigade, consisting of two battalions of slow moving infantry support tanks. They struck the 7th Panzer Division and the SS Totenkopf Division,

Above: Consolidation of the German hold on the Channel coast.

Far left: Many towns were only surrendered after intense street fighting.

Left: A near miss for a Kubelwagen of Rommel's 7th Panzer Division.

Right: How the Dunkirk pocket was formed.

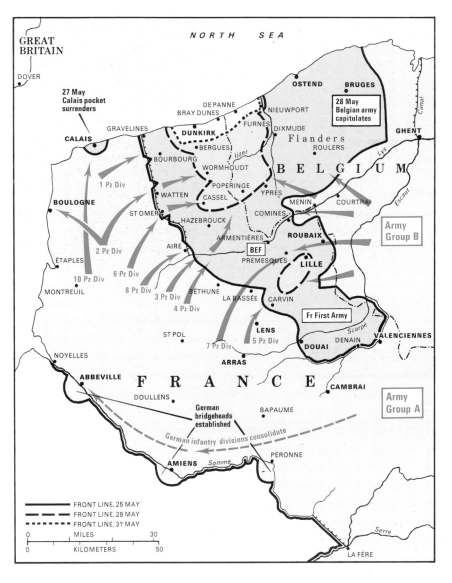

Right: *The tension shows on the faces of these British troops being evacuated from Dunkirk.*

Above: *French troops surrender Lille. That they should be allowed to march out with fixed bayonets is unusual, but showed that chivalry in war was not yet dead.*

Above right: *Erwin Rommel, just after his division had trapped the 51st Highland Division in St Valery-en-Caux, 12 June 1940.*

momentarily knocking them off balance and causing some panic, which reverberated up the German command chain, with von Rundstedt ordering a temporary halt until the situation was resolved. The British tanks, unsupported like de Gaulle's had been earlier, were soon forced to draw off, and on 22 May von Rundstedt was ordered to begin to squeeze the Allies in the pocket in which they were trapped.

The German armor was now beginning to the feel the effects of the past 12 days. Casualties, vehicle breakdowns and the growing exhaustion of the crews prompted von Kleist to request a pause for breath. Von Rundstedt agreed to this, especially since once again it would allow the infantry to catch up. In addition, the terrain in the north-east corner of France was less suitable for armored warfare, being riddled with waterways, and infantry would be needed in greater numbers to assist the tanks. Hitler concurred with this, and only Guderian seems to

have been unhappy. Another element also entered Hitler's planning. Goering believed that the Luftwaffe could finish off the Allied forces in the pocket and Hitler was persuaded to let him have his way.

On 25 May the Belgians, with almost all their country now in German hands, warned their allies that their situation was becoming impossible. Gort realized that, should they surrender, his army stood every chance of being lost as well. Believing that his duty was to save as much as possible in order to fight another day, he arranged with his government for it to be evacuated. This began on the following day, with the now famous armada of small ships making their way across the Channel to bring the troops home. That same day Hitler let the leash off his armor once more, while the Luftwaffe began to pound the Allied forces in the pocket. On the 27th, King Leopold of the Belgians offered to surrender and Goering commented: 'Only fish-

ing smacks are coming across; I hope that the Tommies can swim well.'

In fact, what later became known as the 'Miracle of Dunkirk' enabled no less than 224,000 British and 120,000 French and Belgian troops to be evacuated back to England, although they had to leave behind almost all their equipment and lost some 200 ships of all types. Successful rearguard actions and the fact that the Luftwaffe was operating at extreme range, enabled so many to get away. On 4 June the Germans entered Dunkirk and Winston Churchill, who had replaced Chamberlain as prime minister on 10 May, made the first of his many famous speeches of defiance, ending '. . . we shall never surrender'.

The Germans now turned their attention to the remainder of France. On 5 June Case Red was executed. After initially being held by the French on the Rivers Somme and Aisne, the German Blitzkrieg machine once more gathered momentum. Paris was entered on the 14th and two days later the French decided to seek an armistice. This came into effect on 22 June. Two days before this, Italian troops had entered the southeast of France.

The German attack in the West had been even more devastating than that which had struck Poland. It had taken just six weeks to bring France and the Low Countries under Hitler's thrall and few outside observers gave Britain much chance of surviving on her own. While Poland should have warned the Western Allies of the way in which the Germans intended to fight, May 1940 still found them totally unprepared for it. Too much faith in static defenses and an unwieldy and creaking command and control structure meant that they were unable to react to the high-speed maneuver warfare practised against them. The result was a military disaster of massive proportions. Yet, as has so often happened in war, it was just one campaign and not final defeat.

Top left: Another French town lies in ruins.

Top right: Rommel with General Fortune on his left after the surrender of the 51st Highlanders. This unit had been in the Maginot Line when the German offensive opened.

Above: German infantry pause for breath in Chateau Thierry during the execution of Case Red, the second phase of the overrunning of France.

THE FALL
OF MALAYA
AND
SINGAPORE
1941-2

The Japanese bombing of Pearl Harbor on 7 December 1941 shocked America. For the British, who had been beleaguered for 18 months, it came like manna from heaven. Finally they would have the might of the USA fully behind them, something for which they had striven ever since the fall of France. Yet, America's entry into the war did not bring about an immediate reversal of fortune; rather, the opposite. The first half of 1942 was for the Allies perhaps the darkest part of the war. On the Eastern Front the Germans thrust towards the Caucasus. In North Africa, Rommel also attacked, driving the British Eighth Army back to the gates of Cairo. In the Atlantic the U-boats enjoyed their second 'Happy Time', plundering shipping off the American eastern seaboard. In the Pacific and South-East Asia the picture became even blacker as the Japanese speedily overran one Allied possession after another. For the British the worst disaster in this sorry sequence of events was to be the loss of Malaya and Singapore.

Malaya, with its huge resources of rubber and tin, was a highly prized asset within the British Empire and it is not surprising that Japan, given her grave shortage of natural resources, should covet it. The British had also recognized, after the Great War, the geostrategic importance of Singapore, lying as it did close to the sea routes to the Far East and Australasia. They therefore decided to construct a naval base there to which a fleet could deploy if a threat did develop. At the same time airfields were to be constructed down the Malayan peninsula in order to secure air routes to Australasia. It was not, however, until the mid-1930s that construction work began. The only possible threat was seen as coming from Japan, and the atmosphere of global disarmament which existed in the 1920s, made this unlikely. Besides, there was little government money available for defense expenditure.

In the early 1930s the situation in the Far East changed. The Japanese overran Manchuria, left the League of Nations and threw off the restrictions of the international naval disarmament treaties. Work now began on constructing the naval base. Because the Army did not believe that any thrust down through Malaya was possible, only the threat from the sea was considered and to this end 15-inch and 9.2-inch guns were installed at the base. The RAF also pointed out that torpedo aircraft would be useful and it was agreed that these should also be made part of the defense. The theory was that Singapore should be able to hold out for 70 days, the time it would take for a fleet to arrive from Britain. In the late 1930s, however, the Army began to have second thoughts and

Previous pages: *Japanese infantry during the last phases of the battle for Singapore, and celebrating the final surrender of the island.*

Above: *An Australian anti-tank gun overlooking the Johore Causeway.*

Right: *A burning rubber plantation. The British set fire to their plantations in order to prevent them falling into enemy hands.*

Below: *ABDA Commander-in-Chief Wavell meets US commanders on Java. His appointment was too late to save Singapore.*

Left: *HMS* Prince of Wales *arrives in Singapore, a pitifully small contribution to the island's naval defenses. Captain Leach, her commander (below left) went down with the ship when it was sunk by Japanese torpedo bombers on 10 December 1941.*

believed that amphibious landings on the east coast of Malaya were possible. Consequently a small sum of money was made available to construct a line of defenses in southern Malaya in order to prevent artillery from firing on Singapore Island. It was, however, only partially completed by the early 1940s.

When Britain found herself at war with Germany in 1939 no fleet was sent to Singapore. Indeed, the governor was told that he must now be prepared to stand a seige of 90 days, the revised period of time it would take for a sizeable naval force to arrive. The only reinforcements which were sent were an infantry brigade from India and four bomber squadrons. Yet, there was no undue concern. Britain was not at war with Japan and there was a widespread belief that the Japanese were inferior to the British in every respect. In the late summer of 1940, however, Japan proclaimed her Greater East Asia Co-Prosperity Sphere, the economic blueprint for making good her acute shortage of raw materials by incorporating South-East Asia within her empire. This was followed by the signing of the Tripartite Pact with Italy and Germany at the end of September. As the same time they stationed forces in the north of French Indo-China, something which the Vichy French forces were powerless to resist, as they were when Japanese forces occupied southern Indo-China in July 1941. In April 1941, too, the Japanese signed a non-aggression pact with the Soviet Union, another indicator that the Greater East Asia Co-Prosperity Sphere was no idle daydream.

Throughout 1940 the British authorities in Malaya and Singapore clamored for additional reinforcements as Japanese designs became

more threatening. Little was forthcoming. In part this was because of the threat of German invasion of Britain, but also on account of Churchill giving the Middle East priority over the Far East and his continued belief that Singapore could only be attacked from the sea. In spring 1941 the Australians, who were more conscious of the Japanese threat, decided to send troops to Malaya, and the Japanese machinations in Indo-China began to make the British consider the possibility of an attack on Malaya through Thailand. Consequently, two more Indian divisions were sent to take care of northern Malaya. A plan, Operation MATADOR, was also developed to forestall an attack from this quarter by advancing into southern Thailand in order to deny the Japanese airfields there, as well as the ports of Singora and Patani. In terms of aircraft, though, the defenses were woefully

Above: *Admiral Tom Phillips (right) commanded the naval squadron, Force Z, and died when the* Repulse *was sunk with the* Prince of Wales.

Right: *General Arthur Percival, who was forced to surrender Singapore. Appointed to command the ground forces in Malaya in May 1941, he warned that sizeable reinforcements would be needed, but they eventually arrived far too late.*

Below: *The path of the Japanese advance through Malaya.*

Below right: *Lightly equipped Japanese infantry at a Buddhist shrine.*

short and what types were deployed were obsolescent and would prove no match for the Japanese Zero fighters. As for naval forces, in spite of the argument that their despatch to Singapore would present a powerful deterrent to the Japanese, it was not until October 1941 that the Admiralty finally relented. The battleship *Prince of Wales* and battlecruiser *Repulse* were sent. They were to have been joined by the aircraft carrier *Indomitable*, but she ran aground on trials in the Caribbean. Thus, Force Z was hardly the fleet that the planners had always envisaged being sent to Singapore.

The Japanese plans for the invasion of Malaya were drawn up during 1941. One significant advantage they enjoyed was that there were many Japanese working in Malaya and Singapore and they were able to provide accurate intelligence on the defenses. They quickly identified the fact that Singapore was virtually undefended on the landward side and hence concluded that their attack must come down through Malaya. Given the nature of the terrain here, they made a careful study of jungle warfare and gave their troops a thorough training in

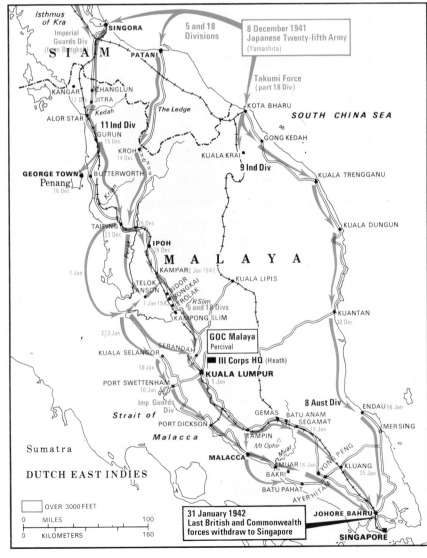

it. This was in contrast to the British, who only paid lip service to this and believed that any thrust must rely on the few roads which ran down through the country. Selected to carry out the invasion was the Twenty-Fifth Army commanded by General Tomoyuki Yamashita. He planned a combined sea and land assault. The Imperial Guards Division would move into Thailand, seize Bangkok and then attack across the border with Malaya. Two regiments of the 5th Division would land at Singora and Patani and then advance south and clear the western side of Malaya, while the 18th Division would land at Kota Bharu and advance down the east coast. Yamashita had a further division, which was still in Japan, which he could call on, and also had the support, if need be, of the Fifteenth Army, which would move into Thailand prior to invading Burma.

On 4 December, as the staff of the Japanese embassy to Washington began to leave and Admiral Nagumo's Pearl Harbor Striking Force moved towards its objective, Yamashita's troops set sail from the port of Hainan in southern China. Two days later an RAF Hudson spotted the Japanese convoy steaming west off the Gulf of Cambodia. The British forces in Malaya were put on the alert, but MATADOR was not put into effect for fear of precipitating a Japanese attack. Although air patrols continued there were no further sightings of the invasion fleet until the afternoon of 7 December. This prompted Air Chief Marshal Brooke-Popham, the overall British commander, to issue a warning order for MATADOR to be mounted on the following day. By then it was too late. At 2.00am on the 8 January 1942 the Japanese landed at Kota Bharu and within two hours had secured a beachhead.

The British deployment in northern Malaya consisted of the 11th Indian Division defending the northwest while the 9th Indian Division covered the east coast, with a brigade at Kota Bharu and another 120 miles to the south at Kuantan. The overall headquarters was that of III Corps, which also had a reserve of one brigade at Ipoh. The south of Malaya was covered by the 8th Australian Division, which also acted as theater reserve. The brigade at Khota Baru launched counter-attacks on the Japanese beachhead and it was also bombed, but to no avail. Then rumors, totally unfounded, that the RAF airfield at Kota Bharu was being attacked resulted in the aircraft there being withdrawn. This enabled the Japanese to land further troops and the Indian brigade consequently withdrew that night. In the meantime the Japanese made unopposed landings at Patani and Singora. They also launched a series of air attacks on the airfields in northern Malaya, destroying a significant number of aircraft on the

ground. Furthermore, in the early hours of the morning two airfields on Singapore Island were bombed, but some aircraft overshot their targets and there were 200 civilian casualties. In spite of all this, it was decided to launch MATADOR, but on a smaller scale than planned. Two battalions, known as Krohcol, crossed the border into Thailand in the early afternoon of the 8th and by last light had penetrated three miles in spite of Thai opposition. A smaller force crossed elsewhere, and advanced nine miles, but then encountered a Japanese column led by tanks. Outflanked, it was forced to withdraw back across the border. Krohcol, however, continued its advance the following day. By mid-afternoon it had reached the town of Betong, seven miles inside Thailand, and Thai resistance ceased. This, however, was the only bright spot of the day. The Japanese had begun to infiltrate out of their beachhead at Kota Bharu and the Indians withdrew well to the south of the town. Worse, the Japanese had now established total air supremacy over northern Malaya. Even so, Krohcol continued its advance on the 10th, its objective the Ledge, a steep ridge 35 miles north of the border. During the afternoon it came up against stiff Japanese

Top: *Abandoned British Bren gun carriers on Singapore Island. Apart from some elderly armored cars, these were the only armored vehicles the British had in Malaya.*

Above: *Japanese troops made much use of bicycles to speed their advance in Malaya.*

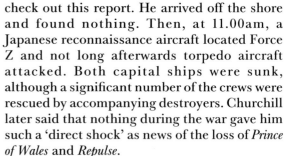

Below: *Japanese troops, far more lightly equipped than their Allied counterparts, make yet another outflanking movement through the jungle. Their superior jungle skills were a significant factor in the British defeat.*

resistance one mile short of the objective. Simultaneously, elements of the Japanese 5th Division crossed the border and the 11th Indian Division covering force fell back on the main defensive position at Jitra.

10 December, however, witnessed the first major disaster of the campaign. When news of the Kota Bharu landings became known, Force Z slipped anchor and sailed north on the evening of the 8th in order to intercept transports bringing in reinforcements to the beachheads in Thailand and at Kota Bharu. On the afternoon of the 9th a Japanese submarine spotted the warships and Japanese aircraft began to shadow Force Z. Warned by the RAF that because of the air situation in northern Malaya air cover for the ships could not be provided, Admiral Phillips, commander of Force Z, decided that evening to return to Singapore. He then received a report of a Japanese landing at Kuantan, 160 miles south of Kota Bharu. Since this was close to his course back to base, he decided to go and

check out this report. He arrived off the shore and found nothing. Then, at 11.00am, a Japanese reconnaissance aircraft located Force Z and not long afterwards torpedo aircraft attacked. Both capital ships were sunk, although a significant number of the crews were rescued by accompanying destroyers. Churchill later said that nothing during the war gave him such a 'direct shock' as news of the loss of *Prince of Wales* and *Repulse*.

During the 11th Krohcol came under increasing pressure, while the Japanese closed up to Jitra and began to advance south from Kota Bharu. But while the British withdrawal on the east coast was orderly, that in the west began to degenerate. On the 12th the Japanese established a lodgement in the Jitra defenses and counter-attacks failed. They then began to feel their way round the flanks of the position and this caused the forward Indian brigade to panic and it fell back to Alor Star on the River Kedah and ten miles to the south. The Japanese, however, were there almost before them, crossed the river that afternoon and precipitated another withdrawal. This pattern was repeated during the next few days. Every time the Japanese came up against opposition on the roads, they immediately took to the jungle, outflanked the position and threatened its rear. By the 17th, Penang Island had been evacuated and 11th Division was continuing to fall back on one river line after another, with Krohcol, having pulled out of Thailand, attempting to guard its right flank. In the meantime desperate requests were made to London for more troops and aircraft.

Yamashita, sensing that his enemy was weakening, was determined to give him no respite and continually urged his troops on. They had little mechanical transport, but did have some tanks (something the British lacked), and their troops relied largely on bicycles. Their physical wants were also very simple, their food being made up largely of rice balls, which meant that logistical support was kept very simple. The Japanese also conscripted Chinese and Malays to repair the airfields in northern Malaya. These were operational once more by 20 December and aircraft from them struck the airfield at Kuala Lumpur on the following day, destroying 12 out of 18 Australian Buffalo fighters. As a result the air commander, Air Vice Marshal Pulford, withdrew the remaining aircraft in Malaya to Singapore, a move which added to the difficulties of the troops defending Malaya.

On the night 22/23 December the 11th Indian Division withdrew across the Perak River, while the 9th Indian Division was given orders to deny Kuantan airfield to the Japanese. 11th Indian Division prepared a main defensive position at Kampar, 30 miles south of Ipoh. During the next week it fought a delaying action back to

Left: *Malay troops and a civilian after a Japanese air raid on a village.*

this position, which the Japanese began to attack on 1 January. For two days they were held, but then news came of a Japanese amphibious landing at the mouth of the Perak River. 9th Indian Division was now under heavy pressure at Kuantan and General Percival, commanding the land forces, ordered it to move west to Jerantut in order to link up with 11th Indian Division, which itself was to fall back to the Slim River. Again, the Japanese were too quick for the defenders. A column led by tanks burst through the defenses north of the river on 7 January and captured the main bridge over it intact. Percival decided that the only option open to him was to concentrate on holding on to Johore, the southernmost of the Malayan states. General Wavell, who had just been appointed commander of the first of the Allied theater commands to be set up, ABDA (American, British, Dutch, Australian), visited Malaya on 8 January and agreed with Percival's latest plan.

On 11 January the Japanese entered Kuala Lumpur and 8th Australian Division became involved in the fighting for the first time. Initially they enjoyed some local successes, especially in terms of well-laid ambushes, but further Japanese landings on the west coast threatened their flank and they were unable to buy the necessary time for a cohesive defense of Johore

to be organized. The British commanders began to turn their attention to Singapore, but in view of the lack of prepared defenses on the landward side Wavell doubted whether the island could be held for any length of time. Churchill,

Below: *Japanese aircrew record details of their last mission. The British totally underestimated the proficiency of Japanese aircraft.*

Above: *A bewildered British soldier is taken into captivity. Many would not survive the next three and one half years in Japanese POW camps.*

Above right: *Japanese troops march past the main post office in Singapore City. The Royal Coat of Arms would soon be removed.*

Right: *The fall of Kuala Lumpur, 11 January 1942.*

however, was adamant. He told Wavell that 'no question of surrender be entertained until after protracted fighting among the ruins of Singapore City'. Thus Wavell ordered Percival to prepare the island for a seige.

On 28 January the withdrawal across the Causeway, which separated Malaya from Singapore, began and was completed three days later. In the meantime, reinforcements in the form of an Indian brigade, Australian troops, and a division from Britain had been landed on the island. Percival thus had the equivalent of some four divisions, well in excess of the Japanese strength, to hold the island. But, morale was low, and was not improved by orders to destroy the naval base, which in British eyes *was* Singapore. There was a serious shortage of weapons. Furthermore, in spite of the presence of a few Hurricane fighters, which had recently arrived on the island, Japanese domination of the air was virtually total.

Yamashita did not attack immediately, mainly because his stocks of artillery ammunition were very low as a result of his rapid advance during the past seven weeks. He therefore paused for a week in order to prepare, but even so he did not have sufficient ammunition for a protracted battle. Percival believed that the Japanese would assault the northeast corner

Right: *The British surrender delegation is escorted through the Japanese lines.*

Below: *British troops in the Malayan jungle, but their training in jungle warfare was all too little.*

Below right: *General Yamashita (center) dictates the surrender terms to Percival (back to camera).*

of the island and laid out his defenses accordingly. His view appeared to be confirmed as correct when the Japanese made a feint landing on the island of Pulua Ubin on the 7th. During the afternoon of the 8th, however, Japanese air and artillery activity suddenly increased in the northwest corner and that night the 5th and 18th Divisions crossed in landing craft. By dawn they had established beachheads and piecemeal counter-attacks made no impression on them.

During the next few days the defenders were gradually pushed back. Wavell made a last visit to Singapore on the 10th, and realized that the writing was on the wall. Yet, on the same day Churchill ordered him to defend the island to the last man, and Wavell passed this on to Percival. He decided, however, that there was nothing to be gained by leaving aircraft on the island and the last of the RAF fighters flew to Sumatra.

The continual Japanese air attacks caused increasing chaos, especially in the docks area, where civilians and military clamored to get on board the last few ships available. It was, however, the growing damage to the public utilities which finally decided the issue. Early on the 14th Percival was told that the water supply on the island was likely to fail. The situation could be improved if counter-attacks were mounted to recapture reservoirs which had fallen to the Japanese, but Percival's subordinate commanders were against this and pessimistic about their ability to resist longer. There was, too, the plight of the one million civilians of all races still on the island. Percival therefore realized that there was no other option. At 11.30am on 15 February a small party of officers approached the Japanese lines with a white flag. Early that evening Percival was taken to Yamashita's HQ to sign the formal surrender.

The overwhelming Japanese victory was but one of a series that they enjoyed during the six months following their attack on Pearl Harbor. It had been achieved largely because of blinkered prewar planning and total underestimation of the enemy. At root was that the British had been taken in by their own propaganda over the impregnability of Singapore. It was an expensive error and the effects of the disaster would be far-reaching. The British standing in South-East Asia would never be quite the same again.

STALINGRAD
1942-3

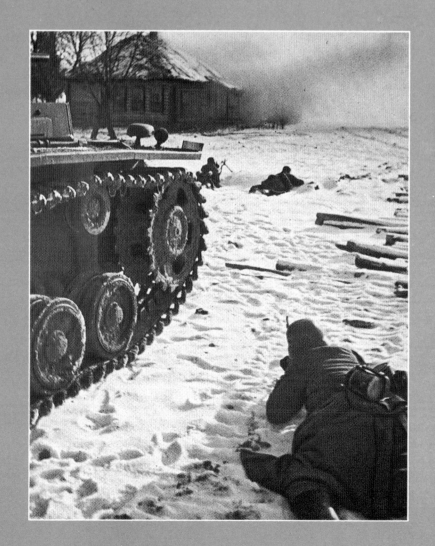

In 1941 the German armies came close to inflicting one of the greatest military disasters of all time, the total defeat of the Soviet armies. That they failed to do so was in part because they were defeated by the Russian winter, but also because Hitler meddled too much in the conduct of operations. Nevertheless, in spite of this failure and subsequent Russian counter-attacks, Hitler remained determined to bring the Soviet Union to its knees.

On 5 April 1942 he issued Directive No 41. The objectives for 1942 were to be the capture of Leningrad, which had been under siege since the previous autumn, clearance of the Crimea, and, above all, overrunning of the industrially rich region between the Rivers Donets and Volga and seizure of the Caucasus oilfields. This was to be carried out by Fedor von Bock's Army Group South, which was to be subdivided into two subordinate commands, Army Groups A (von Weichs) and B (List). Two attacks were to be made. One mounted from north of Kharkov was to be directed southeast in order to clear the area between the Donets and the Don, while well to the south of Kharkov the other headed for the Donets Basin and the north bank of Don. The two drives would then link up and proceed down into the Caucasus. As a subsidiary to this, Stalingrad on the Volga was to be captured in order to secure the left flank of the Caucasus drive.

Stalin and his generals were convinced that the Germans would attack again in front of Moscow, and, in order to pre-empt this, decided to mount an attack of their own. This was to be from a salient which they had created during January-March. Conducted by Semyon Timoshenko's South-West Front, this was launched on 12 May and initially took the Germans by surprise. However, six days later the Germans mounted a counterstroke into the neck of the salient and trapped the Russians, capturing well over 200,000 prisoners by 29 May. This left von Bock free to prepare his own offensive.

The Germans went to great lengths to make the Russians believe what they already thought, that the offensive was to be directed on Moscow. However, on 19 June a German staff officer carrying a copy of the plan was shot down and the plan fell into Russian hands. The Germans made no changes as a result of this security breach and on 28 June the offensive opened. They quickly created a pocket northeast of Kharkov, but captured few Russians, who were careful to withdraw their forces before they could be entrapped. As Army Groups A and B swept southeast between the Don and Donetz, Hitler became increasingly frustrated at von Bock's failure to destroy the Russian armies

and, on 23 July, sacked him. On the same day he ordered List to thrust into the Caucasus while von Weichs advanced east to Stalingrad. This meant that the Germans would now be advancing on two divergent axes and that the offensive as a whole became increasingly difficult logistically as did the provision of air support.

Initially, priority lay with the Caucasus and on 9 August the Germans reached the Maikop oilfields. By then, however, priority of air support had been switched to von Weichs and, in particular, to Friedrich Paulus's Sixth Army, which was being joined by Hermann Hoth's Fourth Panzer Army transferred from Army Group A. On 10 August Paulus crossed the Don and reached the outskirts of Stalingrad. Two weeks later his troops had also closed up to the Volga north of the city.

Hitler had by now become mesmerized by

Previous pages: *Knocked-out Soviet T-34 tanks, during the German 1942 summer offensive, and German defenders of the Stalingrad pocket.*

Top: *Goering, Hitler and Keitel plan the 1942 summer offensive on the eastern Front.*

Above left: *General Friedrich Paulus (left), commander of the ill-fated German Sixth Army.*

Above: *Marshal Semyon Timoshenko, whose thrust south of Kharkov in May 1942 was quickly destroyed.*

Stalingrad, even though List had reached the Caucasus Mountains, and was determined that it should be captured. Yet, Stalin, too, had become equally insistent that the city that bore his name be held and, on 24 August, sent Georgi Zhukov, his troubleshooter, to supervise its defense personally. On 3 September Paulus and Hoth linked up and attempted to break into the city from the west. Limited Russian attacks on their flanks frustrated the Germans, however. Nevertheless, Paulus and Hoth maintained their pressure in what had now become costly street fighting, with the Russians fiercely defending every street and every building. By the beginning of November, the onset of winter and overstretched supply lines had meant that the offensive in the Caucasus had ground to a halt, but Paulus was still butting his head against downtown Stalingrad.

It was now that the Russians launched a double counter-stroke. For some weeks Paulus had been operating in the nose of a salient, the shoulders of which were held by allied formations, the 3rd Rumanian Army in the north and the 4th Rumanian Army in the south. The Russians had noted this and evolved a plan whereby simultaneous attacks would be launched by Vatutin's South-West and Rokossovsky's Don Fronts in the north and Eremenko's Stalingrad Front in the south against these vulnerable flanks, the object being to cut off the German troops fighting in Stalingrad.

On 19 November URANUS, as this operation was codenamed, was launched, with the northern prong of the attack going in first. Initially

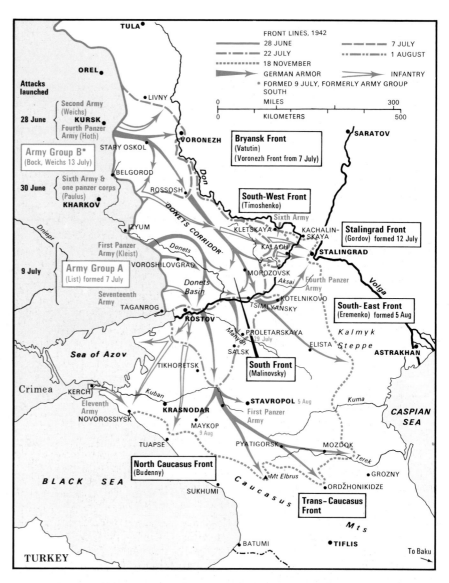

Above: *The increasing commitment of Army Group B towards Stalingrad left Army Group A over-extended in the Caucasus.*

Left: *Tanks of Hermann Hoth's Fourth Panzer Army crossing the Don near Voronezh, July 1942.*

Top: *German artillery in action in the suburbs of Stalingrad during Paulus's initial attempts to capture the city.*

Above: *German engineers constructing a pontoon bridge over the Don.*

the Rumanians put up stiff resistance, but by the end of the second day it had crumbled and Vatutin had penetrated 25 miles. On this day Eremenko attacked in the south, and on the 21st Paulus withdrew his headquarters west to the River Chir in order to maintain contact with the remainder of Army Group B. Hitler, however, countermanded this and ordered him to move back to Gumrak, close to Stalingrad itself. It was clear that nothing would induce Hitler to release his hold on the western part of Stalingrad. On the 22nd Vatutin seized a vital bridge over the Don at Kalach, vital since it was on Paulus's main communications route to the rear. The next day saw the link up between Vatutin and Eremenko. The whole of Sixth Army and part of Fourth Panzer Army, 330,000

men in all, were now cut off, and, with the two Rumanian armies virtually destroyed, separated from the remainder of Army Group B by some 40 miles.

If Hitler did have any doubts of the efficacy of leaving Paulus where he was, these were quickly dispelled by Goering, who stepped in to declare that the Luftwaffe would keep Paulus resupplied. Hitler therefore ordered Sixth Army to stand fast and not to contemplate a break-out. He also organized a new formation, Army Group Don, under Erich von Manstein, with the specific task of mounting a relief operation. Von Manstein wanted to mount this, under the codename WINTER STORM, as soon as possible in order both to achieve maximum surprise and prevent the Russians from consolidating their gains. He was forestalled in this, however, by Russian attacks on the Lower Chir on 30 November. Von Manstein had to deploy a large part of his command to contain these and hence it was not until 12 December that WINTER STORM was launched. In the meantime, the Russians also attempted to split the Stalingrad pocket into two, but without success.

Because of von Manstein's commitments to the Lower Chir he initially had only two Panzer divisions with which to mount WINTER STORM. Even so, by selecting an axis of advance which was not the shortest route to Stalingrad he avoided major resistance. But, a number of river ravines lay in his path and it took time to surmount these. Consequently the Panzer divisions had only penetrated some 20 miles, when on the third day of the operation they were struck by Russian armor and became embroiled

in a three-day tank battle. Worse was to follow.

On 16 December the Russians launched LITTLE SATURN. This was designed to cut von Manstein's relief force off and, as they had done in November, was concentrated against a weak point in the German line, the sector held by the Italian Eighth Army. Parts of Vatutin's South-West and Golikov's Voronezh Fronts. The Italians, however, did resist stoutly and it was not until the third day that a breakthrough was achieved. There was little German armor in the area and, having broken through, the Russian armor raced southwestwards and even succeeded in overrunning Tatsinkaya, the main airfield supply to the Stalingrad pocket. In the meantime Von Manstein's relief force, with a third Panzer division now involved and having finally brushed off the Russian armor, pushed on to the east. Eventually, however, having been forced to give up a Panzer division to deal with the crisis provoked by LITTLE SATURN, and with his tank strength seriously reduced, von Manstein had to withdraw on Christmas Eve in the face of renewed Russian counter-attacks and because his southern flank was now threatened by an assault on Fourth Rumanian Army, which had still not recovered from its drubbing in November. Previously, on 19 December, he had implored Paulus to break out and link up with him, but the Sixth Army commander, conscious of Hitler's order to him, was only prepared to offer some tanks unsupported by infantry. On that same day the Luftwaffe managed to deliver 250 tons of supplies to Stalingrad, its highest daily total, but only a third of what Paulus needed.

Above left: A German mortar detachment approaching the outskirts of Stalingrad.

Above: The Swastika flies over Stalingrad, but the Russian defenders (left) fought so tenaciously that Paulus was unable to capture it all.

Such were the multiple threats to Army Group Don that Hitler was forced to sanction a widescale withdrawal, which by 31 December put it 125 miles away from Stalingrad. This aggravated Paulus's tenuous supply situation still further. Even so, Hitler still believed that relief of Stalingrad was possible. The Russians, however, were determined that it was not to happen.

On 30 December 1942 the Soviet High Command issued orders for the reduction of the

Stalingrad pocket. The task was to be given to Rokossovsky's Don Front, which was now to command seven armies, three transferred from Eremenko's Stalingrad Front (renamed South Front on 1 January 1943). While Eremenko maintained pressure on von Manstein in order to prevent another relief operation, Rokossovsky planned to roll up the pocket from west to east, with just one army, Vassili Chuikov's 62nd, which had been fighting within Stalingrad itself, to apply pressure from the east. Stalin wanted Rokossovsky to launch his final attack on 6 January, but grudgingly agreed to a four day postponement in order to allow more time for deployment and resupply of the attacking armies.

The situation within the pocket itself was becoming increasingly grim. Although the Luftwaffe was doing its best, at an increasing cost in its transport workhorse, the Junkers Ju 52, its average daily deliveries of supplies were now no more than 90 tons. Matters were made even more difficult and hazardous in that only one of the seven landing strips within the pocket had night landing facilities. Rations had to be constantly cut and the intense cold of the Russian winter aggravated hunger. At the end of December one of Paulus's aides wrote to a friend of his in Germany: 'At the moment we are feeling somewhat betrayed and sold out . . . I just want to tell you quite simply that there is nothing to eat, with the exception of a few thousand horses . . . No miracle in the steppe can help us here, only good old Aunt Ju [Ju 52] and the He 111 if they come – and come often.'

On 8 January a Russian *parlementaire* entered the German lines under a white flag with a message from Rokossovsky. It was a surrender demand, with a promise of good treatment for all who did so. Paulus immediately sent a message to Hitler requesting 'freedom of action', especially since he knew that the Russians were about to launch a major assault. Hitler rejected it, sending General Hans Hube into the pocket to tell Paulus that he must hold out since three Panzer divisions were being sent from France and would mount another relief operation in mid-February. Paulus, clutching at this straw, resolved to fight on.

On 10 January Rokossovsky mounted his attack under a concentrated artillery barrage, to which the German guns could make little reply because of their shortage of ammunition. By the end of the day the Russians had penetrated up to five miles. On the 13th the most westerly of the airfields in the pocket, Karpovka, was overrun and three days later, only one airstrip, Gumrak, remained in German hands. In the meantime, in a last desperate effort to improve resupply of the pocket, Hitler despatched Field Marshal Erich Milch, Goering's deputy and a

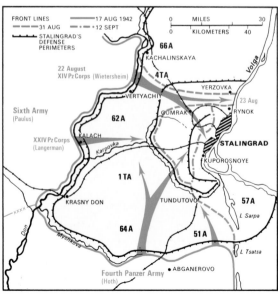

Top: *Goering's empty boast – Ju 52 transports in winter camouflage fly low to evade Russian fighters in their vain efforts to keep the Stalingrad pocket supplied.*

Above: *Stalingrad was gradually reduced to little more than a vast expanse of rubble.*

Left: *Paulus's first attempt to seize Stalingrad.*

Left: *Stukas attacking Russian strongpoints in Stalingrad.*

Below: *Soviet troops overrunning one of the seven airfields within the Stalingrad pocket.*

Left: *A female Soviet soldier, cheerful in the snow, brings in German prisoners.*

Right: *Red Army engineers, equipped with long probes to detonate mines, cutting lanes through German defenses prior to an attack.*

Right: *Attacking Soviet infantry pass a knocked-out German tank.*

Left: *Coping with the winter. German drivers build igloos around their vehicles to protect them from the cold.*

Right: *German light machine gunner on outpost duty. In such temperatures sleep could bring hypothermia and death.*

Far right: *Soviet troops closing in on the last remaining centers of resistance in Stalingrad.*

man with a high reputation as an organizer, to von Manstein's HQ, now at Taganrog. There was little he could do. Gumrak itself was now under shellfire and landing there became increasingly hazardous. Supplies now had to be dropped by parachute, but as often as not they fell inside the Russian lines. Few of the many wounded could be evacuated and many merely froze to death. Yet, in spite of this and the lack of food and ammunition there were still plenty of officers and men prepared to fight on.

On 22 January the final phase of the reduction of the pocket began. Paulus sent Hitler another desperate signal pointing out his grim situation, but was told to fight on. The following day an He 111 took off from Gumrak with 19 wounded and seven bags of mail. It was the last aircraft out of the pocket and shortly afterwards Gumrak itself fell. The Russian 21st Army made contact with Chuikov's men fighting in Stalingrad itself and the German Sixth Army was now reduced to two isolated pockets, one in the north of the city and the other in the south. Paulus himself was in the southern pocket, with his HQ located in the basement of the Univermag department store. Such was the food shortage that he issued orders that from then on no rations were to be given to the sick and wounded, of whom there were now some 30,000. Yet, Hitler remained adamant that Paulus must fight to the last and forbade any attempt to break out, even by small groups of men.

On 30 January Goering spoke to the German people on the anniversary of Hitler's accession to power: 'A thousand years hence Germans will speak of this battle with reverence and awe.' Paulus, too, marked the occasion with a message to his Fuhrer: 'The swastika flag is still flying above Stalingrad. May our battle be an example to the present and coming generations, that they must never capitulate even in a hopeless situation, for then Germany will emerge victorious.' His reward was immediate promotion to Field Marshal, but his vow was to be an empty one.

On the following morning Paulus sent an emissary to the Russians. He was now willing to surrender. The northern pocket continued to resist, mainly in and around a ruined tractor factory, for a further 48 hours, and was eventually subdued by Soviet artillery. Hitler's reaction was: 'This hurts me so much because the heroism of so many soldiers is nullifed by one single characterless weakling.' Announcing the fall of Stalingrad to the German nation, he declared four days of mourning, with all places of public entertainment being closed. Some 91,000 Germans surrendered at Stalingrad, leaving 110,000 of their comrades buried in the snowy wastes of what had been the pocket. Of

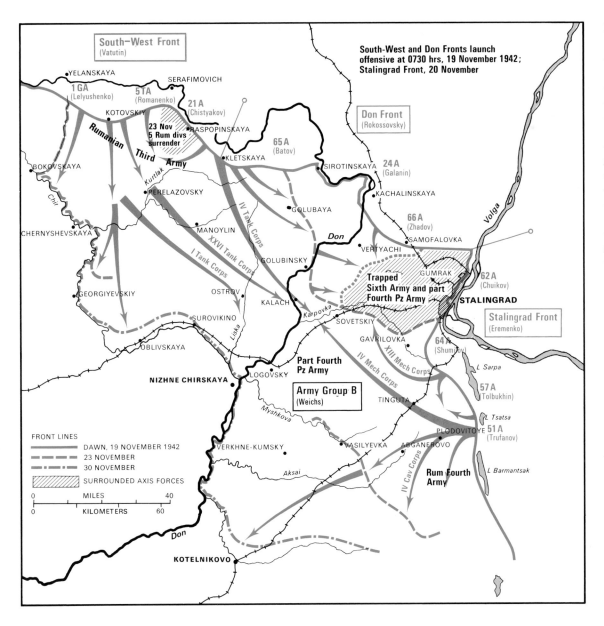

South-West Front
(Vatutin)

• YELANSKAYA

SERAFIMOVICH •

1 GA
(Lelyushenko)

5 TA
(Romanenko)

21 A
(Chistyakov)

KOTOVSKIY •

• RASPOPINSKAYA

23 Nov
5 Rum divs
surrender

Rumanian

Third Army

• KLETSKAYA

65 A
(Batov)

South-West and Don Fronts launch
offensive at 0730 hrs, 19 November 1942;
Stalingrad Front, 20 November

Don Front
(Rokossovsky)

SIROTINSKAYA •

24 A
(Galanin)

KACHALINSKAYA •

Volga

BOKOVSKAYA •

Kurtlak

• PERELAZOVSKY

IV Tank Corps

• GOLUBAYA

66 A
(Zhadov)

SAMOFALOVKA •

Chir

CHERNYSHEVSKAYA •

• MANOYLIN

XXVI Tank Corps

Don

VERTYACHI •

GUMRAK •

62 A
(Chuikov)

• GEORGIYEVSKIY

I Tank Corps

GOLUBINSKY •

Trapped
Sixth Army and part
Fourth Pz Army

STALINGRAD

• OSTROV

Liska

KALACH •

Karpovka

SOVETSKIY •

Stalingrad Front
(Eremenko)

• SUROVIKINO

GAVRILOVKA •

64 A
(Shumilov)

• OBLIVSKAYA

IV Mech Corps

XIII Mech Corps

L Sarpa

Part Fourth
Pz Army

LOGOVSKY •

TINGUTA •

57 A
(Tolbukhin)

NIZHNE CHIRSKAYA

Myshkova

Army Group B
(Weichs)

L Tsatsa

PLODOVITOYE •

51 A
(Trufanov)

• VERKHNE-KUMSKY

• VASILYEVKA

ABGANEROVO •

L Barmantsak

Aksai

IV Cav Corps

Rum Fourth
Army

FRONT LINES

———— DAWN, 19 NOVEMBER 1942

– – – 23 NOVEMBER

–·–·– 30 NOVEMBER

///// SURROUNDED AXIS FORCES

0	MILES	40
0	KILOMETERS	60

Don

KOTELNIKOVO

Far left: *Recalled from China to deal with the war in Russia, General Vasili Chuikov was horrified by the apparent chaos at Stalingrad. His leadership was crucial to the Russian success.*

Below far left: *Newly promoted Field Marshal Paulus is grim-faced after his surrender. Hitler had expected him to commit suicide rather than give in. He later became an active anti-Hitler propagandist for his Soviet captors.*

Above: *How the Soviet offensive created the pocket at Stalingrad.*

Right: *The Soviet triumph is marked by the hoisting of the Red Flag over Stalingrad's main square. It was the turning point of the war on the Eastern Front.*

those who survived only some 5000 would ever return to Germany, and then long after the war was over. Paulus himself, and some of his senior officers, were so disillusioned by what they saw as their betrayal, that the Russians eventually persuaded them to broadcast anti-Hitler propaganda.

The débâcle at Stalingrad marked the major turning point of the war on the Eastern Front. From now on the Germans were on the defensive against an ever more efficient Russian war machine. It was a disaster that could have easily been avoided if it had not been for the obstinacy and myopia of one man, Adolf Hitler.

THE
FALAISE
POCKET
1944

Normandy in summer 1944 witnessed some of the toughest fighting in the West during the Second World War. That it eventually turned out to be disastrous for the Germans was, like Stalingrad, not that they had fought badly, but because their generals were trapped by Hitler in a straitjacket which allowed them no freedom of action.

The Allies had initially been able to establish their beachheads so quickly because Hitler refused to release in time the three divisions which made up the armored reserve in the theater, Panzer Group West. What armor was initially available was committed piecemeal and, because of Allied pressure, found itself holding the line, rather than being concentrated in reserve for counterstrokes. While the overwhelming Allied air supremacy made life difficult enough for the defenders, it was the fire produced by the vast Allied naval armada, especially that from the 15-inch guns of the battleships, which really got them down during the early weeks. Erwin Rommel, commanding Army Group B and directly responsible for conducting the defense, and his superior, Gerd von Rundstedt, Commander-in-Chief West, soon realized that the only way out of their dilemma was to relieve the armor by reserve formations, carry out a limited withdrawal in order to draw the Allies out of range of their naval gunfire and then counter-attack them in the flanks.

Von Rundstedt and Rommel put this proposal to Hitler when he met them at Soissons at 17 June, but he ignored it, his attention being fixed by Cherbourg, which he demanded be held to the last, and the V-1 flying bomb offensive against England, which had opened four days before. The only comfort that the two commanders could take was that further reinforcements, including an SS Panzer Corps, were on their way to the West.

Cherbourg itself was invaded by the Americans on 22 June and its garrison surrendered five days later. Hitler had demanded an armored counterstroke into the rear of the Americans besieging Cherbourg, but was told that it would take two weeks to mount this. Now that the port had fallen Hitler still demanded a counter-attack, and against the Americans, whom he believed to be weaker than the British in the east of the beachhead. The British pressure on Caen, however, was so extreme that all available forces were needed here and none could be spared. Once again von Rundstedt and Rommel demanded to be allowed to withdraw their forces. Hitler's answer was to summon them both immediately to his Alpine retreat at Berchtesgaden at the end of the month.

Again, Hitler refused to listen to them, con-

tinuing to harp over the 'miracle weapons' which would dramatically alter the course of the war. It was clear, however, that they could now expect little more in the way of reinforcements since the long awaited Soviet summer offensive had now begun and the back of Army Group Center was being broken. Worse, on their return to France on 30 June they were greeted with another demand from Hitler that not only were they not to surrender any ground, but that they were to mount an immediate counter-attack against Montgomery's latest attack in the eastern part of the beachhead, EPSOM. For von Rundstedt it was the last straw and he re-

Above: *Three of the leading lights of 12th SS (Hitler Youth) Division, which gave the Canadians such a hard time – (l to r) Kurt 'Panzer' Meyer (captured 6 September while commanding the Division), Fritz Witt (killed 16 June, while commanding the Division), Max Wünsche (badly wounded and captured during the Falaise fighting).*

Left: *Gerd von Rundstedt, CinC West until his dismissal on 2 July 1944.*

Above right: *British troops rehearsing the Normandy landings.*

Right: *The Allied breakout and creation of the Falaise Pocket.*

Previous pages: *American M18 Hellcat tank destroyer and its crew in a newly-liberated French town, late summer 1944.*

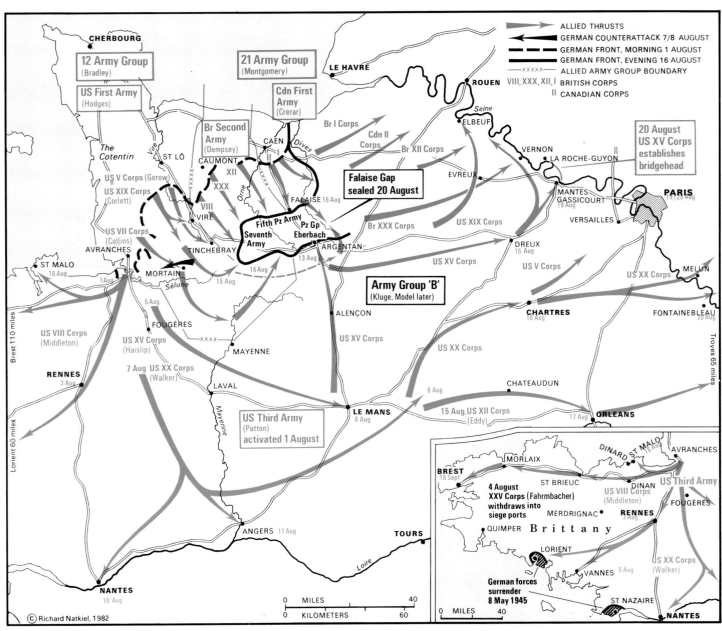

ALLIED THRUSTS
GERMAN COUNTERATTACK 7/8 AUGUST
GERMAN FRONT, MORNING 1 AUGUST
GERMAN FRONT, EVENING 16 AUGUST
ALLIED ARMY GROUP BOUNDARY
VIII, XXX, XII, I BRITISH CORPS
II CANADIAN CORPS

CHERBOURG

12 Army Group
(Bradley)

US First Army
(Hodges)

21 Army Group
(Montgomery)

LE HAVRE

Cdn First Army
(Crerar)

ROUEN

Seine

ELBEUF

Br I Corps

Cdn II Corps

Br XII Corps

VERNON

LA ROCHE-GUYON

**20 August
US XV Corps
establishes
bridgehead**

The Cotentin

ST LÔ

Br Second Army
(Dempsey)

CAEN

Dives

EVREUX

MANTES
GASSICOURT

PARIS

CAUMONT

XII

**Falaise Gap
sealed 20 August**

US V Corps (Gerow)

US XIX Corps
(Corlett)

XXX

Orne

FALAISE 16 Aug

VIII

VIRE

**Fifth Pz Army
Seventh Army**

**Pz Gp
Eberbach**

Br XXX Corps

US XIX Corps

VERSAILLES

US VII Corps
(Collins)

TINCHEBRAY

ARGENTAN

DREUX
16 Aug

US V Corps

US XX Corps

MELUN

AVRANCHES

ST MALO
16 Aug

MORTAIN

1 Aug

Sélune

13 Aug

16 Aug

15 Aug

Army Group 'B'
(Kluge, Model later)

US XV Corps

CHARTRES
16 Aug

FONTAINEBLEAU
20 Aug

Brest 110 miles

5 Aug

FOUGÈRES

ALENÇON

US XV Corps

Troyes 65 miles

US VIII Corps
(Middleton)

US XV Corps
(Haislip)

xxxx

MAYENNE

US XX Corps

CHATEAUDUN

Lorient 60 miles

RENNES
3 Aug

7 Aug US XX Corps
(Walker)

LAVAL

Mayenne

LE MANS
8 Aug

6 Aug

15 Aug, US XII Corps
(Eddy)

ORLEANS
17 Aug

US Third Army
(Patton)
activated 1 August

ANGERS 11 Aug

TOURS

Loire

NANTES
10 Aug

0   MILES   40

0   KILOMETERS   60

© Richard Natkiel, 1982

DINARD ST MALO

AVRANCHES

BREST
18 Sept

MORLAIX

ST BRIEUC

DINAN

US Third Army

**4 August
XXV Corps (Fahrmbacher)
withdraws into
siege ports**

US VIII Corps
(Middleton)

FOUGÈRES

MERDRIGNAC

RENNES
3 Aug

QUIMPER **B r i t t a n y**

LORIENT

VANNES
5 Aug

US XX Corps
(Walker)

**German forces
surrender
8 May 1945**

ST NAZAIRE

0   MILES   40

NANTES

Above: *Preparations for the ill-fated counterattack at Mortain.*

Left: *Goering inspects the damage done by von Stauffenburg's briefcase bomb at Hitler's HQ in the East, the Wolf's Lair, on 20 July 1944.*

Above right: *Some of the defenders of Hitler's much vaunted Atlantic Wall – members of the Indian National Army recruited largely from disaffected Indians captured in North Africa.*

signed his command, using the pretext of his health.

Von Rundstedt's successor was Hans von Kluge, recently recovered from a serious motor accident on the Eastern Front. Having been 'brainwashed' by Hitler, he arrived on the Western Front imbued with an unreal optimism about the situation. Indeed, he roundly rebuked Rommel in front of his staff for his gloomy view of the situation which he represented at their first meeting. Von Kluge, however, very quickly realized that Rommel was right and that to allow the troops in Normandy to continue to be pounded where they were would gain nothing. Even so, the German troops on the ground continued to resist fiercely. This was true especially on the approaches to Caen, which had been designated an objective to be achieved by the end of D-Day itself. This area was fanatically defended by the 12th SS Panzergrenadier Division (Hitler Youth) in the face of continued British and Canadian assaults. These forced the Germans to draw the bulk of their armor away from the Americans, especially after Montgomery's armored thrust east of Caen, GOODWOOD, which took place 18-20 July.

Two significant events happened at this time, however. The first occurred on 17 July when Rommel was seriously wounded by a marauding Allied fighter while returning to his headquarters. Three days later, and far away at Hitler's headquarters at Rastenburg in East Prussia, a bomb exploded in the room in which he was holding one of his conferences. This immediately triggered an attempted military coup in Berlin and the arrest of SS and Gestapo men in Paris. The plot failed because Hitler survived the explosion and tables were very quickly turned on those involved with it. Rommel and von Kluge were both implicated to the degree that they were intending to initiate negotiations with the Western Allies, but von Kluge refused to openly declare his hand on 20 July itself. In any event, having assumed command of Army Group B as well as his theater command, he was too embroiled in military events in Normandy to take any active part.

The shift of the German Panzer formations to the eastern part of Normandy inevitably weakened the forces opposing the Americans and created the conditions for finally breaking out of the beachhead. On 25 July General Omar Bradley's US First Army attacked south towards Avranches under the codeword COBRA. Within 36 hours the back of the German defenses in this sector had been broken. Avranches was liberated and the Americans then swung east. In order to continue to keep the maximum number of German troops tied down in the east, the British then mounted Operation BLUECOAT on 30 July.

By 1 August the pressure had become so severe on the Germans that they had almost reached breaking point. On this day, Bradley, now promoted to command the newly formed US 12th Army Group, released George S Patton's US Third Army, which had been secretly gathering in Normandy, to overrun Brittany and south towards the River Loire. This had the effect of turning the left flank of SS General Paul Hausser's German Seventh Army, which was opposing the Americans. Pressed, too, from the

Above: *Omar Bradley, commanding US 12th Army Group, is visited by Supreme Allied Commander Dwight Eisenhower, August 1944.*

north by the US First Army, now commanded by Courtney Hodges, and the British, the danger of it becoming trapped now loomed. Hitler admamantly still refused to countenance any voluntary withdrawal and even went as far as sending General Walter Warlimont to von Kluge to emphasize the point. He then went further, ordering a counter-attack into the open flank of the American drive south.

Von Kluge was too weak to resist this demand, but instead of waiting until he had concentrated all his available armor, he merely collected what was immediately available, three Panzer divisions, or, at least, the remains of them, since they totalled only 145 tanks. They attacked at midnight on the night 6/7 August, but were immediately delayed by an Allied fighter-bomber, which crashed on to the lead tank of a battalion in a narrow defile, therefore blocking the route. Early morning fog helped and by noon on the 7th an advance of several miles towards Avranches had been made. Once the fog had cleared, however, the Allies could deploy their massive airpower, and rocket-firing

aircraft were soon in abundance over the battle-field. Later the Allied air forces claimed a large number of tanks destroyed. Most, however, had been abandoned by their panic-stricken crews, and the attack came to an abrupt halt. That evening von Kluge, whose heart had never been in it, called it off.

That night the Canadians attacked south-wards from Caen in Operation TOTALISE. The object was to cut off the German Seventh Army. Initially the attack was successful; the infantry division holding the line broke under prepara-tory bombardment by over 1000 RAF bombers. The SS Hitler Youth Division, which was rest-ing after its efforts around Caen, was sum-moned to restore the situation and hurriedly constructed a new defense line to the rear, which brought the Canadian attack to a halt. In the meantime, Patton's armor had overrun most of Brittany and, besides closing up to the Loire, had also turned east, with General Wade Haislip's XV Corps liberating Le Mans on the 8th. Patton now ordered Haislip north, which further increased the threat to Hausser's army.

Above: *US troops coming ashore in Normandy, 6 June 1944.*

Above right: *Erwin Rommel.*

Right: *German light machine gun crew guard against Allied invasion.*

Previous pages, main picture: *British Sherman Firely with 17 pdr gun, during the fighting on the Normandy beachhead.*

Inset: *M4 Shermans pass through a battle-scarred French village.*

Above: *American P-51 Mustangs in the skies over France. Allied supremacy was virtually total.*

Hausser himself was only too well aware of the worsening situation, as was SS General Sepp Dietrich, newly appointed to command Panzer Group West, which had now been re-titled Fifth Panzer Army. They strongly represented their views to von Kluge, but he had now been ordered by Hitler to renew the counter-attack in the Avranches area. For this purpose he had formed a special headquarters under General Heinrich Eberbach, former commander of Panzer Group West, to coordinate it. With Haislip now threatening to sever Hausser's communications, it was too late to renew the attack towards Avranches and Eberbach now planned to forestall Haislip at Alençon,

especially since Hausser's main supply route ran through this town. The Americans, however, moved too quickly for him and seized Alençon on the 12th.

Montgomery, believing that the Germans would resist more fiercely in the Alençon area than against the Canadians in the north, even though TOTALISE had stalled, ordered the Americans to advance north to just south of Argentan and drew a boundary between the British 21st Army Group and US 12th Army Group here. At the same time he told the Canadians to renew their efforts and advance to Falaise and then Argentan. The Canadians, however, who had been halted eight miles short

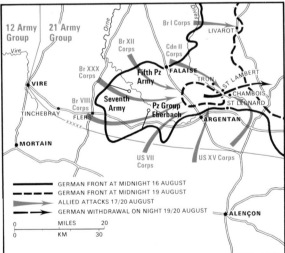

Top: *The Allied air threat forced German road traffic to employ many air sentries.*

Above right: *How the Falaise Gap was eventually closed.*

of Falaise, were unable to resume their attack until the 14th. In the meantime, Haislip had been ordered north and, in optimistic mood, asked Patton if he could advance north of Argentan until he met the Canadians. Patton agreed, but, as it happened, on the 13th Haislip did run into stiff resistance south of Argentan. The reason for this was that von Kluge had finally woken up to the fact that Hausser was about to be totally trapped and Eberbach's three Panzer divisions, having been too late to influence events at Alençon, had now moved to the Argentan area. Even so, Patton was confident that, with the Canadians still not moving, he could close the gap. He was therefore aghast

to receive an order from Bradley on the afternoon of 13 August telling him that on no account was Haislip to advance north of Argentan. According to Patton, the reason given to him was that the British had dropped delayed action mines north of Argentan from the air, but the truth was that Haislip had already crossed the inter-army group boundary and Bradley did not want to risk the Allies firing on each other.

The Canadians renewed their attack on the 14th, but suffered an initial setback when, because of a target marking mistake, RAF Bomber Command dropped bombs on their forward troops. The SS defenders managed to hold the Canadians on the River Laison until the afternoon, but were then forced back. It was not, however, until the evening of the 16th that Falaise was entered, such was the fierceness of the resistance. Indeed, one Hitler Youth detachment held out in the town high school for a further three days.

Within the Falaise pocket itself life had become increasingly impossible. Pounded from the air and also by Allied artillery, casualties had been mounting at an ever increasing rate. All the same, Hitler still insisted on no withdrawals. Eventually, however, on the 14th von Kluge had realized that if he was to save anything he must give the order to withdraw and gave Hausser an optimistic five days to extricate his men. He spent most of the next day cowering in a ditch and out of contact after his car had

Above: *Waffen-SS Panzergrenadiers, one armed with a captured US carbine, move through the bocage.*

Right: *British troops, including an Armoured Vehicle Royal Engineers (AVRE), in Normandy.*

Above right: *SS Gen Sepp Dietrich, who commanded Fifth Panzer and Seventh Armies during the last phase of the Normandy battle.*

Left: *Bren Gun carriers cross the Seine at Vernon during the British breakout which culminated in the liberation of Brussels.*

Below: *Patton, Bradley and Montgomery enjoying a rare moment of harmony together. So frustrated was Patton at not being allowed to close the Falaise Gap on his own that he threatened to drive the British into the sea and create a 'second Dunkirk'.*

Left: *Clearing the Falaise Pocket – GIs pass a knocked out PzKw IV.*

Above: *British commandos and paratroopers, who held the extreme left flank of the Allied beachhead in Normandy.*

been shot up by Allied fighters. On the 16th, Hitler, believing that von Kluge had been trying to negotiate with the Allies, ordered him back to Germany, replacing him by Walter Model, who was then on the Eastern Front.

Meanwhile, Hausser's men struggled eastwards through the narrow gap between Falaise and Argentan, a gap which I SS Panzer Corps in the north and Eberbach's Panzer divisions in the south struggled desperately to keep open.

On 17 August the Canadians began to push southeast of Falaise. The pocket itself now began to be squeezed by the British Second Army from the north and west and elements of the US First Army from the south. In the meantime, the bulk of Patton's Third Army had already begun to race for the Seine.

Model himself arrived in France on the 18th and immediately saw that Normandy was lost. He hoped to be able to set up a new defensive line west of the Seine and ordered Dietrich to establish it from the coast to south of Paris.

Above far left: *Some of the carnage inside the Falaise Pocket.*

Below far left: *An exhausted MG42 machinegunner, one of the defenders of Caen.*

Above left: *German tank driver.*

Top: *A wounded and mentally shattered Waffen-SS man surrenders.*

Above: *Walter Model arrived too late to save more than mere remnants of the German armies in Normandy.*

The Canadians, largely because of the inexperience of their troops, continued to advance slowly and it was not until the 21st that they finally met the Americans at Chambois. Next day the Allies concluded that all the Germans left in the pocket were either dead or captured. Those who now went into it were aghast at the destruction that had been wreaked. One American officer wrote: 'As far as the eye could reach . . . on every line of sight, there were vehicles, wagons, tanks, guns, prime movers, sedans, rolling kitchens, etc., in various stages of destruction . . . I stepped over hundreds of rifles in the mud and saw hundreds more stacked along sheds . . . I saw probably 300 field pieces and tanks, mounting large caliber guns, that were apparently undamaged.' In all, some 50,000 were captured and another 10,000 killed in the pocket. Army Group B was left with no more than 70 tanks and Fifth Panzer and Seventh Armies were now mere skeletons.

Falaise was undoubtedly a disaster for the Germans and would have been an even worse one had it been sealed earlier. Even so, the ten days that followed the closing of the pocket gave the impression that the German armies in the West were totally broken and that there was a very real prospect of total Allied victory for the end of 1944. Paris was liberated and the Allied armored spearheads broke out across the Seine, liberating large tracts of northern France. In the south of France, too, where Allied forces had landed on 15 August, progress was dramatic. The high point came with the liberation of Brussels by the British on 3 September, but then the tanks ground to a halt. They were out of fuel. Hitler's phobia over voluntarily giving up terrain did prove to be sound in one respect. He had declared the French Atlantic and Channel ports as *Festungen* (fortresses), which were to be held to the last man. This denied their use to the Allies, who were forced to continue to rely on the Normandy coast for bringing in their supplies. Consequently, their high-speed advance across northern France so stretched the supply lines that they eventually snapped. Their forced halt enabled the German armies to recover and condemned the Allies to a long and hard fall nd winter. Thus the disaster that befell the Germans in August 1944 was only temporary, although the very landings in Normandy itself did mark the beginning of the end.

THE GREAT
MARIANAS
TURKEY
SHOOT
1944

llied fortunes in the Pacific began to turn with the battles of the Coral Sea and Midway in the early summer of 1942, actions in which the aircraft carrier finally confirmed its dominance in the war at sea. The Americans now evolved a strategy of 'island hopping'. This entailed a series of amphibious operations, beginning with the landings on Guadalcanal in the Solomon Islands in August 1942, designed to bring them ever closer to their ultimate objective, the Japanese mainland. By the late summer of 1943 this strategy had evolved into two major drives. While General Douglas MacArthur's South-West Pacific Area and Admiral William Halsey's South Pacific Area cleared the New Guinea coast and the Bismarck Archipelago, Admiral Chester Nimitz's Central Pacific Area would begin to advance from Pearl Harbor to regain the clusters of Pacific islands that lay en route to the Philippines. Both drives would then combine to secure the Philippines themselves.

The Japanese, faced by these multiple threats to their newly acquired empire and realizing that everywhere their forces were stretched too thin, were now forced to rethink their strategy. They decided that they must shorten their vast perimeter. Consequently, under the 'New Operational Policy', they decided to concentrate on the defense of the line Burma – Malaya – western New Guinea – Carolines – Marianas – Kuriles. All territory which they held outside this line would merely be used to buy time for the minimum area of defense, as defined above, to be made impregnable. They were also determined to step up warship and combat aircraft production in order to be able once more to

Above: *Roosevelt, seated between Douglas MacArthur and the President's personal chief of staff, Adm William Leahy, is briefed by Adm Chester Nimitz on the situation in the central Pacific.*

Right: *How the opposing fleets took up position in the Philippine Sea.*

Above: *Adm Chester Nimitz, who conducted the island hopping campaign across the central Pacific.*

Above right: *Adm Raymond Spruance (left), whose Central Pacific (later Fifth) US Fleet fought the Battle of the Philippine Sea, with Nimitz, April 1944.*

Above far right: *Recording Japanese aircraft shot down by a US destroyer.*

Right: *Adm Marc Mitscher, perhaps the most outstanding of the US carrier force commanders, on the bridge of USS* Lexington. *His Task Force 58 played the lead role in the Turkey Shoot.*

challenge the dominance of US naval power.

During the latter part of 1943 the Allies continued the clearance of the Solomon Islands and made landings on New Britain, while Nimitz began his Pacific drive with successful amphibious assaults against Tarawa and Makin in the Gilberts, followed in January and February 1944 by landings in the Marshalls. He now looked west towards his next objectives, the island of Truk, 1500 miles to the west, and the Marianas, approximately the same distance northwest of Truk.

As the American successes mounted so the Japanese looked increasingly to the Navy to restore their fortunes. Commander-in-Chief of the Combined Fleet Admiral Mineichi Koga, who had succeeded Yamamoto, mastermind of the Pearl Harbor attack, after he had been shot down by a US fighter over Bougainville in April 1943, was a conservative by nature. Yet he harbored a dream of a decisive naval victory, like that at the Tsushima Straits 40 years before, which would dramatically alter the war situation. Consequently, he had reorganized the Combined Fleet around the carrier force, with the battleships relegated to the role of support. During 1943 four more escort carriers had been commissioned as against just one lost in action. Koga was also killed in an air crash in April 1944, but not as a result of enemy action. On 2 May, the day before his successor, Admiral Toyoda, was officially appointed, the Navy Staff issued an order: 'All forces are to be prepared to meet the enemy in the area of his main offensive and, with one blow, destroy the enemy fleet and thus thwart his offensive plans.'

Toyoda's problem was to decide where the Americans would strike next. There appeared to be three possibilities, judging from current US naval activity. These were the Marianas, the Palau Islands, which lay east of the Philippines, or somewhere north of Australia, the latter two options reflecting a thrust towards the Philippines depending on whether it was made to the east or west of New Guinea. Toyoda therefore decided to place his main fleet, the carriers with their attendant battleships, off North Borneo. This could react quickly to the two Philippines options and Borneo also had large stocks of oil, a commodity that was becoming ever scarcer for the Japanese. In addition, he utilized the islands on the defensive perimeter as static aircraft carriers, deploying over 1600 aircraft to the Marianas, Carolines, and Iwo Jima, which lies some way to the north of the Marianas, as well as to the Palau Islands. These would strike the first blows, while the main body of the fleet moved in and finished off the Americans.

The Americans, in the meantime, were continuing their steady advance. While MacArthur and Halsey secured the Bismarck Archipelago, which isolated the main Japanese base at Rabaul, and cleared the north New Guinea coast, Nimitz began his operations for the capture of the Marianas. His first action was to begin softening up his objectives and to this end carrier-launched air strikes were flown against the Marianas and Truk from February onwards. Truk, the main Japanese naval base in the Pacific, was destroyed by air attacks at the end of April and the Japanese forced to evacuate it. This removed the threat both to Nimitz, and Halsey and MacArthur.

The force with which Nimitz now intended to seize the Marianas was the largest so far gathered in the Pacific. It consisted of three elements. The first was the landing force, made up of three Marine and one US Army divisions, with no less than 12 escort carriers, five battleships and 11 cruisers. The carrier task force, Admiral Marc Mitscher's TF58, which had been carrying out the preliminary bombardments, boasted 15 carriers and 900 aircraft. Finally, in support, was Admiral Raymond Spruance's US Fifth Fleet, with seven battleships and 21 cruisers. In carriers alone, the Japanese, who had only nine, were totally outnumbered and the only true advantage that they enjoyed was that their aircraft had a greater range. Nimitz planned to assault Saipan, the largest of the islands, first and then land on Tinian and Guam to its south. His troops would land on the west side of Saipan since the defenses were likely to be less strong than on the east coast. His invasion fleet set sail from Hawaii and on 11 June

Far left: *An F6F Grumman Hellcat fighterbomber is catapulted off the carrier* Monterey *during the Philippine Sea battle.*

Below: *A US B-24 Liberator bomber during an attack on a Japanese-held Pacific island.*

Left: *Mitscher's Task Force 58 prior to the Battle of the Philippine Sea.*

Far left: *A ship's Curtiss SC-1 floatplane, which was used for reconnaissance.*

Left: *US Marines land on Saipan in the Marianas, 15 June 1944. In the background smoke from the naval bombardment hangs over the island.*

Mitscher's aircraft began their softening up, striking Saipan and Tinian and leaving over one hundred Japanese aircraft completely destroyed on the ground.

During the past two weeks, however, Toyoda had had his attention diverted elsewhere. On 27 May, the anniversary of the Battle of the Tsushima Straits, MacArthur's troops had landed on the island of Biak off the northwest of New Guinea. This took Toyoda and his staff by surprise. His chief of staff, Admiral Kusaka, however, saw an opportunity to bring the US Pacific Fleet to battle by mounting an operation to retake Biak. He was convinced that this would draw the Americans in and that they could be engaged in the area of the Palau Islands. Consequently, reinforcements were hastily collected together and on the night 8/9 June the Japanese attempted to land them on Biak from destroyers. They were, however, intercepted by an Allied naval squadron and put to flight before they could do so. Now, with the air attacks on Saipan and Tinian, Toyoda realized that he had been looking in the wrong direction and his carriers were 2000 miles away. Nevertheless, he ordered Admiral Ozawa, commanding the main body, to steam immediately for the Marianas.

On 13 June the US battleships and cruisers began to bombard Saipan and Tinian. The Japanese, now realizing that the landings were going to come in from the west, hastily adjusted their defenses. Then, on the morning of the 15th, the 2nd and 4th US Marine Divisions went ashore on Saipan. Although resistance on the beaches was fierce, by nightfall the Marines had consolidated their beachheads and 20,000 men were ashore. A Japanese counter-attack that night made no impression and further landings were made the following day.

On hearing of the landings, Toyoda immediately radioed Ozawa, ordering him to attack the US fleet and annihilate it. He then repeated Admiral Togo's famous signal at Tsushima: 'The fate of the empire depends on this battle. Let every man do his utmost.' Ozawa himself, although he realized that his fleet was numerically inferior, believed that he could win. He intended to take maximum advantage of his aircraft's greater range, launching them against

Above: *The Japanese carriers* Unryu *(top) and* Taiho *(above).* Taiho *was sunk on the first day of the battle after being torpedoed by a US submarine.*

the Americans while the distance between the fleets was too far for the Americans to strike back. They would then refuel and rearm on Guam before attacking again en route back to the carriers. He also counted on using the land-based aircraft in the Marianas, not realizing that most of these had now been destroyed. On 18 June his aircraft first located the US carriers west of Saipan, but, in spite of the desire of some of his subordinate commanders to attack immediately, Ozawa resolved to wait for the morrow. Hopes that his presence remained undetected by the Americans were, however, to prove false. Thanks to their ability to read the Japanese top secret ciphers (Magic), they were well aware that the main body had left North Borneo and US submarines had been monitoring its progress through the San Bernardino Strait in the Philippines and on to the Marianas. Mitscher was therefore well aware of the presence of the Japanese fleet and wanted to sally forth and attack it. He was, however, forbidden to do so by Spruance, who was mindful of his prime duty to support the landings on the Marianas. He, like the Japanese, also remembered the Tsushima Straits, and how Togo had waited for the Russians to come to him.

Dawn off the Marianas on 19 June brought squalls and cloud. It was thus not until 0730 hours that Ozawa's reconnaissance aircraft

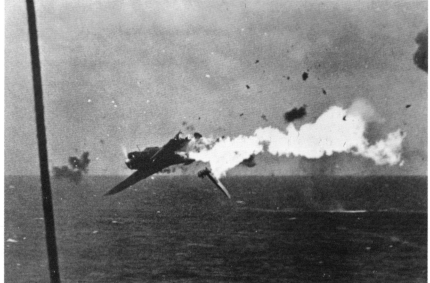

once more located Mitscher's carriers, now southwest of Saipan. Ozawa immediately ordered the launch of his aircraft. The first wave of 71 took off, followed just under half an hour later by another wave of 126. Just after the second wave had taken off, one of its pilots noticed the track of a torpedo racing towards Ozawa's flagship, the 33,000 ton carrier *Taiho*. He immediately dived on it and sacrificed his own life in intercepting it. The US submarine *Albacore* which had fired it also launched another

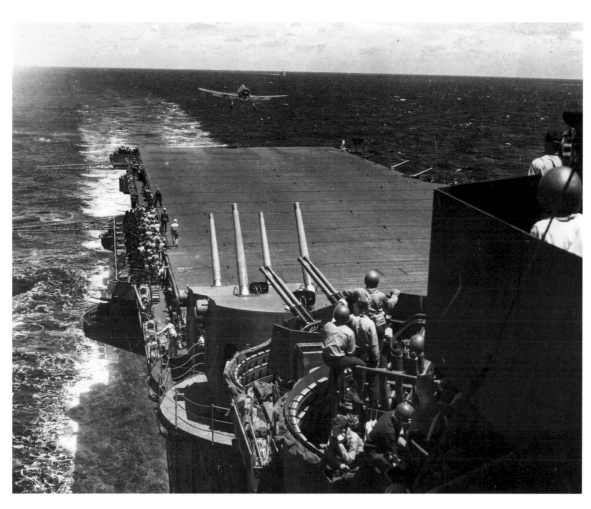

Above far left: *US Marines just after hitting the beach on Saipan.*

Below left: *A US carrier's guns have done for this Japanese torpedo-bomber.*

Left: *USS* Lexington *recovers one of her Hellcats during the battle.*

Below: *The course of the two-day Battle of the Philippine Sea.*

and this struck the *Taiho* in her starboard side. Although Ozawa did not at first believe it, it was to be a mortal blow.

It was at 10.00am that American radars first detected the incoming Japanese aircraft. The carriers were alerted and swarms of heavily armed and armored Grumman F6F Hellcats began to take off. Meeting the first Japanese wave, they quickly shot down one third of it.

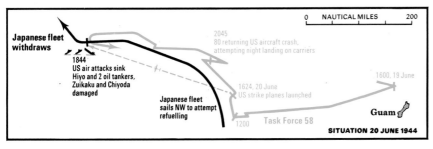

The remainder pressed on, meeting further Hellcats and suffering more losses. Eventually, only one Japanese aircraft managed to get through, striking the battleship *South Dakota*. The second Japanese wave suffered the same treatment, losing almost 70 of its number. The Japanese had also launched two additional waves, but these had been misdirected and the majority of the few which reached the target were also shot down. The remainder, having jettisoned their bombs, flew on to Guam, but further Hellcats were waiting for them and shot down another 30, as well as badly damaging many others. In all, no less than 346 Japanese aircraft, 80 percent of Ozawa's strength, were lost that morning. In contrast, 15 US aircraft were downed. Worse, another US submarine, *Cavalla*, lcoated the carrier *Shokaku*, firing six torpedoes at her, three of which struck and quickly sank her. Thirty minutes later, the *Taiho* was ripped apart by an internal explosion, caused by her damage control officer opening all her ventilation ducts, which allowed gasoline fumes to permeate the ship. Ozawa, though, had by then transferred his flag to the *Oyoda* and now gave orders for the force to withdraw.

The Japanese steamed northwest. Ozawa, probably assuming that most of his aircraft had landed on Guam, intended to refuel and continue the battle on the following day. His oppo-

nent, Mitscher, believing that the Japanese were on their knees, was determined to capitalise on his success immediately. This time Spruance allowed him his head, and Mitscher set out in pursuit with three out of his four carrier groups. The shadowing US submarines had withdrawn after making their successful attacks on the carriers and, hence, Mitscher had to deduce the direction in which Ozawa had withdrawn. As it happened, he guessed wrong and set off on a southwest course. It was not until late the following afternoon that a US aircraft eventually located the Japanese carriers. Mitscher knew that he only had a few hours of daylight left, but decided, none the less, to take a gamble.

Turning his carriers into the wind he launched 216 aircraft. The first target they sighted was a collection of six oilers. Some aicraft attacked these, sinking two, while the remainder pressed on to tackle the main target, the carriers. These managed to get 75 aircraft into the air, virtually all that were left on board after the actions of the previous day, and these, supported by the ships' guns, managed to account for some 20 US aircraft. The others, however, were undeterred and pressed on, striking and damaging the carrier *Zuikaku*, which Ozawa had now made his flagship, the light car-

rier *Chiyoda*, a battleship and a light cruiser. Worse, the carrier *Hiyo* was struck by two torpedoes, burst into flames, and quickly settled. The US aircraft then turned for home amid the gathering darkness. Their flight back to the carriers was, however, fraught with difficulty. Unused to navigating by night, a number lost

Left: *Some of the many ships which supported the landings on Saipan.*

Below left: *The Japanese carrier* Zuikaku *and her two attendant destroyers desperately try to evade an air attack. She was, however, damaged.*

Right: *A Japanese aircraft burns in the sea after narrowly missing this US carrier.*

themselves and others ran out of fuel. Eventually, Mitscher was forced to switch his carriers' lights on, in spite of the danger that this might attract Japanese submarines, and most of the pilots were able to land. With only 35 aircraft left on board his carriers, Ozawa realized that he had nothing left with which to continue the battle. He therefore made use of the darkness to set course for Okinawa. Deeply conscious of the fact that, instead of achieving another Tsushima, he had suffered a major defeat, he penned a letter of resignation to Toyoda, who believing that the reverse was more his responsibility, refused to accept it. The Battle of the Philippine Sea, to give the action its official title, was, however, largely responsible for the resignation of the government of General Hideki Tojo, which took place a month later. It was Tojo who had been largely instrumental in bringing his country into the war, but criticism of his strategy had been growing and Ozawa's defeat and the fall of Saipan, which was eventually secured on 7 July, were the last straws.

The American aircrew who took part in the destruction of Ozawa's aircraft termed it 'the Great Marianas Turkey Shoot', an apt description of the slaughter. Yet, the disaster to the Japanese was not so much the 475 aircraft, including some 50 based on Guam, which were lost during the two-day battle. It was not even the sunk and damaged aircraft carriers. Indeed, the world's largest aircraft carrier, the 71,890 ton converted battleship *Shinano*, was currently nearing completion at the Yokosuka Navy Yard. Primarily, it was the loss of so many aircrew, who could not be replaced in the same way as ships and aircraft. It was this that meant that never again could the Japanese Imperial Navy put to sea with a balanced fleet, and which forced it to resort to a last desperate measure, the *Kamikaze* or suicide aircraft. In other words, the Battle of the Philippine Sea broke the back of Japanese naval airpower.

Above: *Results of the preparatory air attacks against Japanese airfields on Tinian.*

DIEN BIEN PHU
1954

When the Japanese surrendered in September 1945 those European nations – Britain, France and the Netherlands – who had built colonial empires in South-East Asia moved to regain control of their territories in the region. They assumed that the clock would automatically be turned back to prior to the outbreak of war in 1941 and that the indigenous peoples would welcome their return. This was not to be the case.

Allied reverses in the early part of the war against Japan had reduced the standing of the European in Asian eyes and there was a wide-scale demand for self-determination. This was fueled by a dramatic spread of Communism, which had been exported from China well before the war. Much of the most effective active resistance to the Japanese during the war in South-East Asia had been by Communist groups. With Mao Tse-Tung's victory over Chiang Kai-Shek in China in 1949, Communism would achieve even greater prominence in the region. The result of all this was that very quickly after the end of the war the European powers would find themselves embroiled in counter-insurgency operations – the Dutch in the Dutch East Indies, the British in Malaya, and the French in Indo-China.

In some parts of South-East Asia the war came to an end so suddenly (because of the dropping of the atomic bombs on Japan) that

Allied forces were in no position immediately to secure colonial territories and oversee the disarming of the Japanese troops which had been occupying them. This was especially so in Indo-China, where a hardened Communist leader, Ho Chi Minh declared independence on 2 September 1945. It was, in fact, the British who were first on the scene, with an Indian Army division sent from Burma. This arrived in Saigon on 11 September and set about disarming the

Previous pages: *French Foreign Legionnaires under Viet Minh bombardment at Dien Bein Dhu.*

Left: *Ho Chi Minh, the Viet Minh leader. He spent time in both England and France as a young man and then many years in China, returning to Indo-China in 1941. He lived to create the republic of North Vietnam, but died in 1969, before his dream of a unified communist Vietnam was realized.*

Below: *Viet Minh troops take over Haiphong during the French withdrawal following the 1954 Geneva Conference.*

Left: *A US-built M24 Chaffee tank supports French native troops in one of the many clearance operations in the Red River Delta.*

Below: *Gen de Lattre de Tassigny visiting a Vietnamese hill tribe in the company of the French installed Emperor Bao Dai of Indo-China.*

Japanese, releasing the French troops held by them, and generally restoring law and order. Likewise Chinese Nationalist forces moved into northern Indo-China. They, however, left Ho Chi Minh's Viet Minh forces alone in their Hanoi base, merely contenting themselves with disarming and repatriating the Japanese troops.

France, because of the ravages of the war, was unable herself immediately to re-establish her authority over Indo-China. Indeed, although the first French troops arrived in Saigon in November 1945, it was not until May 1946 that they were in a position to begin to reclaim the country. Even so, they were only able to secure the southern half of what is now Vietnam, together with Cambodia and Laos. Once the Nationalist Chinese had left northern Indo-China, the French entered into negotiations with Ho Chi Minh. They were, however, only prepared to offer a measure of limited independence under the nominal leadership of the non-Communist Emperor Bao Dai, which did not suit the Viet Minh. Consequently, towards the end of 1946 French forces occupied Haiphong and Hanoi and demanded that the Viet Minh surrender its arms. The latter refused to do so and hence the French moved to occupy northern Indo-China by force. During the period December 1946 – March 1947 they established control over the towns and cities in the north and the Viet Minh withdrew to the hinterland of the mountainous Viet Bac area by the border with China and the Red River delta.

During the next three years the French remained very much on the defensive, seeking to consolidate their hold on the towns and lowland areas of the north by establishing garrisons and setting up defensive lines. Their offensive

Right: *Viet Minh troops in Hanoi in late 1954, after the French withdrawal from Indo-China. Much of their weaponry came from China.*

operations, drives into the hinterland, were limited in nature and merely reaction to acts of terrorism. This suited the Viet Minh, giving them the opportunity to build up their strength, both in terms of men and weapons. Ho was especially helped in procurement of the latter after Mao's victory over Chiang Kai-Shek in 1949. Ho Chi Minh also did much to rally support among the peasants of the rural areas.

By mid-1950 the Viet Minh military commander, General Vo Nguyen Giap had organized a force of 40,000 regulars in four divisions and felt strong enough to present a more

Right: *The French empire in Indo-China and the 1954 division of Vietnam. The inability of the Vichy French regime to resist Japanese pressure during 1941-5 and the political vacuum at the end of World War 2 gave Ho Chi Minh the opportunity to organize his campaign.*

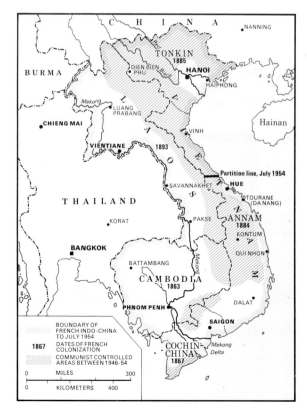

bellicose military challenge to the French. In a series of surprise attacks he cleared the French out of northern Tonkin province and even threatened both Hanoi and Haiphong. So shaken were the French that in December of that year they sent out their leading soldier, Jean de Lattre de Tassigny, to restore the situation. He had commanded the French First Army during the 1944-5 campaign in Northwest Europe and had after the war risen to command the Allied land forces in Western Europe.

De Lattre quickly set about restoring morale and tore up plans to evacuate the Tonkin Delta area, constructing a further series of defenses there. This was timely, since it was here that Giap intended to strike next. This he did in January 1951, only to be bloodily repulsed. Two further attempts in March and May with the same result cost Giap 20,000 men. Accordingly, he withdrew once more to the hinterland to lick his wounds. De Lattre, however, succumbed to cancer and returned, at the end of the year, to France, to be replaced by the more cautious General Raoul Salan. He was merely content to consolidate de Lattre's success in the Delta and did little to regain northern Tonkin. This enabled Giap not only to restore his strength, but to increase it to six divisions. Furthermore, he was able to obtain a significant amount of artillery, both field and anti-aircraft, from the Chinese. Accordingly, Giap still continued to test the French. In the fall of 1952 his forces overran the area between the Red and Black Rivers. In Operation LORRAINE the French attempted to regain this area, but without much success. However, Giap became over-confident and repeatedly and unsuccessfully attacked a French garrison at Na San in December. Although he was puzzled by this reverse, he was undeterred.

Above: *French and Vietnamese questioning refugees. As the Americans were to find a decade later, these often included Communist agents.*

Above right: *French paratroopers on an offensive patrol designed to interdict the Viet Minh supply lines in the Dien Bien Phu area.*

Right: *French and Vietnamese troops on an anti-Viet Minh drive southwest of Hanoi, autumn 1953. This gives a good idea of the terrain over which much of the war was fought.*

Below right: *Viet Minh Soviet-built M1938 122mm howitzer. Supplied by the Communist Chinese and manhandled through the jungle, it was guns like these which surprised the French at Dien Bien Phu.*

Right: *A French officer points out positions to his Viet Minh counterparts during the French withdrawal from North Vietnam, late 1954.*

Below: *French and native troops during an operation designed to eradicate Viet Minh bases near Hanoi, January 1954.*

Above far right: *Paratroopers dropping to reinforce the garrison at Dien Bien Phu.*

Below far right: *A wounded man being carried to safety after a Viet Minh artillery barrage on Dien Bien Phu.*

In April 1953 the Viet Minh invaded Laos. After some initial success, Giap outran his supplies and was forced to withdraw, leaving a small force behind to keep the French there occupied.

Because of the seeming stalemate, Salan was replaced in May 1953 by General Henri Navarre, a cavalryman who had commanded a division in Algeria. He arrived with instructions from Paris to appraise the situation and make his recommendations. At the time he arrived in Indo-China the French ground forces in the theater consisted of 175,000 men, including Vietnamese troops, but 100,000 of these were committed to virtually static posts. The Viet Minh, on the other hand, had a main force of 125,000 men, supported by 75,000 Regional troops and up to 350,000 largely untrained militia elements. The main Viet Minh threats appeared to be to the Tonkin Delta and northern Laos. Navarre concluded that the latter was the more difficult to counter. His proposal was to divide the theater into two zones, north and south. In the north the French would spend the campaign season 1953-4 on the defensive, but would launch spoiling attacks to dislocate Giap's offensive preparations. In the south the French would go on to the offensive in Annam and Central Highlands. They would also carry out a pacification campaign in the Tonkin Delta and build up the Vietnamese Army. These two measures, combined with reinforcements sent from France, would enable Navarre to build up sufficient mobile forces to engage Giap in open battle during 1954-55, that is after the 1954 monsoon season.

Navarre took this plan back to France, where it had a lukewarm reception. He was promised only a fraction of the reinforcements he had re-

quested and some American aid, but with strings attached. The truth of the matter was that the French nation's heart was not in maintaining France's Far East empire and was merely looking for an easy way to obtain an honorable withdrawal. Even so, Navarre was expected to achieve military success, and quickly.

Navarre had set his plan in motion before he flew to France. The first operation, which involved an airborne landing close to the border with China, was very successful. Some 5000 tons of supplies were destroyed before the paratroopers made for the coast to be recovered by the French Navy. The next, at the end of July in Annam, was designed to destroy a Viet Minh regiment, but failed. Navarre then ordered the evacuation of the isolated fortified camp at Na San, scene of Salan's successful action the previous December. This again was highly successful, with the Viet Minh not realizing what was happening until it was too late. Navarre was also prompted to carry out this operation because of intelligence received that Giap's offensive was aimed at the Tonkin Delta. Consequently, Navarre concentrated his avilable forces in this area and during the autumn harried the Viet Minh there sufficiently to derail Giap's plan.

Navarre now turned his attention to the defense of northern Laos and it was now that the village of Dien Bien Phu came into play. This is situated some 180 miles west of Hanoi and had been occupied by the Viet Minh in November 1952. Navarre saw this as a possible forward mounting base for an invasion of northern Loas and believed that by seizing it he could prevent this. The success of his airborne operations and the successful evacuation of Na San

convinced him that there would be little difficulty in both seizing the objective and, if necessary, extricating his forces. Furthermore, such a
blow would invite the Viet Minh to attack and
be slaughtered.

Operation CASTOR, as it was called, was
mounted on 20 November 1953. Two parachute
battalions dropped on Dien Bien Phu, taking
the Viet Minh there completely by surprise.
They were quickly driven out, and a third
French battalion dropped in the early afternoon. Three further parachute battalions and
some heavy equipment were delivered on the
next day, and the force, under the overall command of General René Cogny set about constructing a series of strongpoints around the village, together with two airstrips.

During the next three months Cogny continued to strengthen his defenses, but also carried out a series of operations designed to har-
rass Giap's supply lines. These were, however,
largely unsuccessful. In the meantime, Giap
had been formulating his own plans. The
French had another base, which they had held
for some time, at Lai Chau, 40 miles north of
Dien Bien Phu. If Giap generated a major threat
in northwest Vietnam, Navarre would be likely
to abandon Lai Chau and hold on to Dien Bien
Phu. Accordingly, he decided to threaten both
simultaneously. Elements of two divisions were
sent against Lai Chau, but no less than three
divisions were ordered to proceed to Dien Bien
Phu. The French became aware of this plan
through radio intercepts towards the end of
November, but were not sure whether complete
divisions were being deployed, or merely elements of them. They tended to believe the latter
because of the logistical difficulties of supporting larger forces.

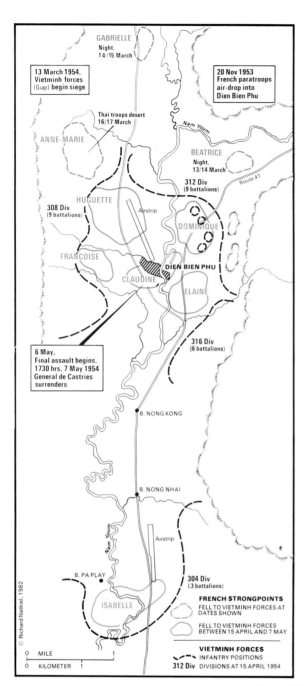

Above: *French wounded being evacuated from Dien Bien Phu before the siege began.*

Below: *A French counterattack. The concept of an aggressive defense was not enough to offset the Viet Minh numerical superiority.*

On 29 November, however, some significant events occurred. Firstly, a Swiss newspaper published an interview with Ho Chi Minh in which he declared his willingness to enter into armistice negotiations provided that the French respected Vietnam's independence. This took the French government by surprise, but Navarre believed that it was because the Viet Minh realized that the French forces would be infinitely stronger come the fall of 1954. Whatever the motivation behind Ho Chi Minh's announcement, it was clear that, if either side achieved a significant military victory, its hand at the negotiating table would be that much stronger. Navarre himself visited Dien Bien Phu on that very same day, 29 November. Inspecting the fortifications in the narrow valley he conceived a new defensive scheme to which he believed the Viet Minh would have no answer. Because the French artillery was confident of neutralizing what limited number of guns Giap would probably be able to deploy, it followed that the main threat would be from infantry. Consequently, a mobile defense based on light tanks could achieve a much more spectacular outcome than one based merely on static fortifications. Accordingly, he selected a new garrison commander, whom he was confident would be able to conduct this type of operation. This was a fellow cavalryman and protégé of Navarre's, Colonel Christian de Castries.

De Castries assumed command of Dien Bien Phu on 8 December. On the same day Cogny ordered the evacuation of Lai Chau, now clearly in danger of becoming isolated. Most of the garrison was flown out by air, leaving a large force of guerrillas to destroy the stocks held there. This left Lai Chau on the following day bound for Dien Bien Phu, but few of its members survived the journey and a force sent from Dien Bien Phu to link up with the guerrillas was itself

Above: *The siege of Dien Bien Phu. The main weakness was that the defensive perimeter was too long for the number of available defenders and some of the strongpoints were too isolated.*

attacked and forced back to its base. This did not bode well for the French.

Navarre, having reorganized the defense of Dien Bien Phu to his satisfaction, now switched his attention to the offensive part of his overall plan, the cleansing of Annam in the south. Giap, too, also intended to mount offensive guerrilla operations here and elsewhere in Indo-China, as well as to launch major attacks on French positions in Laos and the Central Highlands. In this way he would keep the French so tied down that they would not be able to reinforce Dien Bien Phu, for it was here that Giap intended to fight the decisive battle. He began this wave of offensive operations just before Christmas and soon nullified the French offensive, which was launched in January. In the meantime he continued to build up and strengthen his supply lines towards Dien Bien Phu.

By 13 March, when the Viet Minh opened their attack on Dien Bien Phu, they had concentrated 50,000 men in the area, supported by some 60 guns and heavy mortars, which were positioned in the hills overlooking the village. In contrast, the French had a mere 13,000 men. During that day the Viet Minh artillery bombarded vulnerable parts of the camp. The French artillery was unable to make an effective reply. In the early evening the Viet Minh attacked strongpoint Beatrice on the northeast perimeter. Totally outnumbered by the attackers and disorganized by the artillery fire, the defense collapsed, and by midnight it was in Viet Minh hands. The following day strong-

Top: *A French command post inside one of the strongpoints at Dien Bien Phu.*

Above: *How the Viet Minh supply lines were maintained.*

Left: *Wounded defenders of Dien Bien Phu. Eventually artillery domination of the airstrips made it impossible to evacuate them.*

point Gabrielle in the extreme north was similarly isolated and captured. The same applied to strongpoint Anne-Marie, just north of the northern airstrip, on the 15th. Thus, in three days the Viet Minh made significant inroads into the defenses and made it virtually impossible to fly in supplies and evacuate the wounded. Such was the shock of this that the French artillery commander, ashamed that his guns had been unable to neutralize the Viet Minh artillery, committed suicide and de Castries' chief of staff had a nervous breakdown.

There was now a two week lull while Giap brought in reinforcements to make good the heavy losses he had suffered. The French parachuted in supplies and some additional troops, but it was clear that they had already lost the battle. Even so, morale among the defenders of Dien Bien Phu remained surprisingly high.

On 30 March the Viet Minh attacked again, this time initially concentrating on the two strongpoints to the east of the village, Dominique and Elaine. They overran half of each, as well as part of Huguette on the west side, penetrating on to the northern airstrip. French casualties were high, but their resistance remained stiff and Viet Minh losses were heavy. It was this that encouraged Cogny to parachute in

yet more reserves. This took place on the night 10/11 April, but 40 percent of the 850 men who dropped did so immediately into Viet Minh hands.

It was now that the monsoon broke, but this was of no help to the French. The low cloud hindered air resupply and gave cover to the Viet Minh as they gradually nibbled away at the remaining defenses. General Cogny now set about organizing a relief force, but Navarre was

Above: Wounded Viet Minh captured by the French at Dien Bien Phu.

Below: A French outpost awaits the next Viet Minh attack.

Left: *The survivors of the garrison at Dien Bien Phu are marched into captivity. Already undernourished, many would not survive the subsequent hardships in Viet Minh prison camps.*

Above: *Some of the booty captured by the Viet Minh. Eventually it was General Giap's ability to maintain his supply lines, even after the monsoon broke, and at the same time deny the French the use of their airstrips at Dien Bien Phu, which forced de Castries to surrender.*

lukewarm to the idea. Consequently, not until the end of April did it begin to move and then only in half the strength that Cogny had hoped for. By then Giap had brought up all his available reserves and additional artillery ammunition. He was now in a hurry to finish off the job, especially since an international conference at Geneva was about to consider the future of Indo-China.

On 1 May the final phase of the seige began. The Viet Minh attacked Elaine, Huguette and Isabelle, the southernmost strongpoint. The fighting was desperate, but gradually the French were forced back, until by the morning of 7 May only scattered pockets of resistance remained. That evening de Castries surrendered to save his troops further bloodshed. They had already suffered 9000 casualties, and just 7000 men were left to march away to Viet Minh prisoner-of-war camps, an experience that many would not survive. The Viet Minh themselves had had 8000 killed and 15,000 wounded.

Although the war would continue for another three months, the disaster at Dien Bien Phu sealed the French fate. Over-optimism, combined with under-estimation of the enemy, and only lukewarm support from the French government and people had been the causes. The last-named would bring about a growing disillusion among the ranks of the more professional elements of the French Army, who felt betrayed. Subsequent events in Algeria, where the French Army was next called upon to fight, were to accentuate this and bring about an abortive mutiny. As for Indo-China itself the Viet Minh defeat of the French gave them control of North Vietnam, but did not bring an end to the conflict in the region, a conflict which still rumbles on nearly 40 years later.

SINAI
1956

In the years since 1945 one of the major trouble spots in the world has been the Middle East. Indeed, the Gulf War of 1991 is just the latest of many conflicts which have taken place in the region. Much of the tension has been centered on Israel and her fight for survival against the Arab states that border her on three sides.

The state of Israel itself was born amid the conflict between Arab and Jew over possession of Palestine, which had been a British mandate since after the end of the First World War. A growing influx of Jewish immigrants before 1939 who regarded the territory as their ancestral homeland, had sparked off a revolt by the indigenous Arabs. This only came to an end with the outbreak of the Second World War. In 1945 the horrors of the Holocaust in Europe prompted many Jews who had survived to seek a new life in Palestine, but the British, who hoped that Jew and Arab would be able to co-exist, imposed a severe restriction on the number of Jewish immigrants that they would allow in. Jewish underground organizations, however, managed to smuggle many in, and also set about trying to drive the British out through a campaign of terror. Eventually, the British referred the problem to the United Nations, who recommended that Palestine be split into two independent states, Jewish and Arab. While the Jews generally welcomed this, the Arabs did not and violence between the two and against the British increased. Even so, the UN General Assembly approved the plan and it was agreed that the British mandate would end in May 1948. They would withdraw all their troops by the beginning of August.

With the ending of the mandate, the Jews, immediately proclaimed the state of Israel. The Arab League, representing the Arab nations, immediately deployed troops to Palestine and the first Arab-Israeli war erupted. In spite of numerous UN imposed ceasefires, this war would continue until early 1949. At the outset the infant Israeli state, heavily outnumbered, lacking weapons, and hemmed in on almost all sides, appeared to stand little chance of survival. Indeed, during the first month's fighting, before the first of the UN ceasefires, much of Israel was overrun. The Israelis decided that defense was the best form of attack and, helped by the ceasefires, which enabled them to acquire weaponry from sympathizers abroad, one by one defeated the forces ranged against them. Indeed, such was their success that by the end of the war they controlled well over two-thirds of Palestine, much more than what had been allotted to them by the UN. This meant that the prospect of forming a Palestinian Arab state had vanished and the Palestinian Arabs became refugees, some under Egyptian rule in

Previous pages: *Israeli-French built AMX-13 light tanks.*

Left: *Moshe Dayan, with his distinctive eye patch, with Gen Dan Tolkowsky (left), commander of the Israeli Air Force.*

Below: *Israeli troops with a portrait of Nasser, found after the capture of Rafah.*

Left: *Israeli signals unit. Given Israel's limited population, women have always played a more active role in the armed forces than in other nations.*

Above: *Soviet-built T-34/85 tanks parading in Cairo. By 1956 the Egyptians had received large amounts of arms from Czechoslovakia, although they still relied to a degree on old British equipment.*

Left: *More Israeli AMX-13s. By the mid-1950s France was Israel's main supplier of arms.*

Above: *Gamel Abdel Nasser. Curiously, his military defeat in 1956 raised his standing in the Arab world.*

Right: *Sinai and Suez 1956 showing the Israeli advance across the desert.*

the so-called Gaza Strip, and the remainder under Jordan on the west bank of the River Jordan. They and the Arab nations, who refused to recognize Israel, harbored a deep canker of resentment over their defeat.

During the next few years this Arab resentment manifested itself internally as well as externally, with successful coups d'etat taking place in a number of Arab countries. These were organized by nationalist elements in the countries concerned – Egypt, Jordan, Syria. They were determined to rid themselves of the Western influence that had dominated their affairs for so long and which, through arms supplies, they believed to be propping up Israel. The last straw came in 1955 when Britain, in an attempt to maintain her influence over the region, formed the Baghdad Pact with Turkey, Iraq, and Pakistan. Egypt formed a joint military command with Syria and made extensive arms purchases from Czechoslovakia. She also formally recognized the Chinese People's Republic, something which Western nations had not yet done, and seemed to be moving fast into the arms of the Communist bloc.

Israel felt threatened by both these events and increasingly irritated by Egypt's refusal to allow her shipping to use the Gulf of Aqaba in order to reach the Israeli port of Eilat at its head. Matters were made worse when Jordan joined the Arab joint military command in 1956.

Israel, however, had some consolation in that she drew closer to France, who was angered by Egyptian support for the independence movement against French rule in Algeria. France now became Israel's main arms supplier.

Throughout the first half of the 1950s Israel's borders were never totally at peace. There were constant minor clashes with her Arab neighbors and Israel's armed forces mounted a number of retaliatory raids which grew from company- to brigade-sized missions. All this served to reinforce Israel's belief that her Arab neighbors

Above: *US-built Harvard trainers of the Israeli Air Force.*

Left: *Port Said, November 1956, showing some of the ships used by the Egyptians to block the Suez Canal.*

Below: *A brewed-up Egyptian T-34 in Sinai.*

Bottom: *Dayan, with Abraham Yoffe (in beret), who commanded the advance down the Gulf of Aqaba, inspecting the captors of Sharm el Sheikh.*

were preparing to attack and destroy her.

At the end of July 1956 events in the Middle East took a dramatic new turn. President Nasser of Egypt declared that he was nationalizing the Suez Canal, which had been run by the British and French since its opening in 1869. He also forbade Israeli shipping from using the Canal. This further irritated Israel, but the British and French, not believing that the Egyptians possessed the technical expertise to run the Canal, resolved to regain control of it by force, force that neither had available immediately. The Americans, viewing this as yet another example of European imperialism, would not support it and proposed through the UN that an international organization run the Canal. Nasser, however, refused to countenance this. Secret Anglo-French preparations for regaining the Canal therefore continued. In September the French told the Israelis what was being planned and this provoked them to take the initiative and act themselves. They would launch a pre-emptive strike on Egypt.

The forthcoming battlefield of the Sinai peninsula was bounded in the north by the Gaza Strip, which abutted into Israel's Mediterranean coastal region. The area here and in northern Sinai as a whole is low-lying desert. The center and south are generally hilly, the highest peak being Mount Sinai (7500 ft), which

Above: *An Israeli P-51 Mustang overflies advancing troops in Sinai.*

Above right: *An Israeli armored column, led by a Super Sherman with French 76.2mm gun.*

lies some 40 miles north of the peninsula's southern tip at Sharm el Sheikh. Approaches to the Suez Canal through this area are restricted to three passes, reading from north to south, Khatmia, Giddi and Mitla.

The Israeli Defense Force under General Moshe Dayan had available for a strike on Egyptian Sinai some 40,000 men organized into ten brigades (one armored, two mechanized, six infantry, one parachute). They had some 200 tanks, mainly US Shermans and French AMX-13s, and were supported by 116 aircraft. Again, a number of these were World War Two piston-engined types, but they did have 60, more modern jets, largely French. With this force Dayan was tasked to destroy guerrilla bases in the Gaza Strip and on the Sinai border, to frustrate Egyptian plans to invade Israel by destroying bases and the logistics infrastructure in Sinai, and to open the Gulf of Aqaba to Israeli shipping.

The Egyptian forces in Sinai were weakened in the late summer and early autumn of 1956 by redeployment to face the growing Anglo-French threat. Consequently, they had left two infantry divisions, an armored brigade and what was called the Light Mobile Frontier Force. The Gaza Strip was held by the 8th Palestinian Division, while the 3rd Infantry Division was based on the El Arish – Abu Ageila area, with one brigade detached to between the Suez Canal and Mitla Pass. The armored brigade, which possessed Soviet T-34 tanks, SU-100 tank des-

troyers, and a motorized infantry battalion, was in reserve west of Abu Ageila. The remainder of the border area was patrolled by the Light Mobile Frontier Force in its jeeps and personnel carriers.

The Israelis realized that, to achieve their objectives, surprise was vital, as well as the early disruption of Egyptian command, control and communications in Sinai. Accordingly, Dayan decided on the daring initial move of dropping a parachute battalion at the east end of the Mitla Pass, using the remainder of the airborne brigade as a link-up force. He hoped that the Egyptians would merely regard this as a retaliatory raid. Two brigades would strike at Rafa, thus sealing off the Gaza Strip, which would be reduced by two other brigades. One brigade would advance down the east coast of Sinai to Sharm el Sheik, while the remainder of the force broke through in the Abu Ageila area.

The Israeli mobilization began on 26 October in strict secrecy. It was, however, helped by the fact that earlier in the month there had been a clash on the Jordanian border, resulting in an Israeli attack on a Jordanian fort. An Iraqi division prepared to move into Jordan to give support and it looked as though Israel might attack here. Consequently it was here that international attention was largely focused rather than on Sinai.

At 1500 hours on 29 October four elderly P-51 Mustangs crossed the border from Israel and proceeded to cut all the Egyptian overhead tele-

Top: *Advanced guard of the Israeli airborne brigade during the link-up operation with the paratroopers dropped at the entrance to the Mitla Pass.*

Above: *5 November 1956. British paratroopers landing on Gamil airfield outside Port Said.*

Left: *Ex-British Sexton 25-pdr self-propelled gun/howitzers, in Israeli service. They were employed with the armored brigades.*

Below: The various Israeli thrusts. The heaviest fighting of the campaign was in the Abu Ageila area.

Below right: An Israeli field artillery unit, with towed 25-pdr gun/howitzers.

phone wires in Sinai. Two hours later the parachute battalion dropped east of the Mitla Pass and the rest of the airborne brigade crossed the frontier and quickly overran the border town of Kuntilla. At much the same time the Israeli forces began their advance towards Abu Ageila. The initial Egyptian reaction was to order the brigade positioned to the west of the Mitla Pass to move up into it and clear the Israeli paratroopers out. On the following day the airborne brigade continued its dash across Sinai, linking up with its detached parachute battalion which was still east of the Mitla Pass, late that night. The advance against Abu Ageila did not go quite so smoothly. An attack by armor from the northwest was beaten back by anti-tank gun fire, but another task force managed, by the end of the day, to find an unguarded defile, which brought it round to the west of Abu Ageila. A further armored task force was deployed to

ward off possible counter-attacks by the Egyptian armored brigade.

On 31 October the Anglo-French air forces began to attack military targets inside Egypt, which served to increase command and control difficulties for the Egyptians. Shortly after dawn the Israeli armored task force which had managed to get west of Abu Ageila the previous day attacked and surprised its defenders. As a result Abu Ageila was quickly overrun, but the Israelis now came under heavy fire from other strongpoints in the area. At the same time Egyptian armor appeared from the north, but was repulsed by a combination of tank fire and close air support. Shortly after this reports were received that the Egyptian 1st Armored Brigade was advancing towards Abu Ageila from Bir Gifgafa. Israeli armor was sent to counter it, but the Israeli Air Force struck first, inflicting heavy casualties. As a result, the remainder withdrew

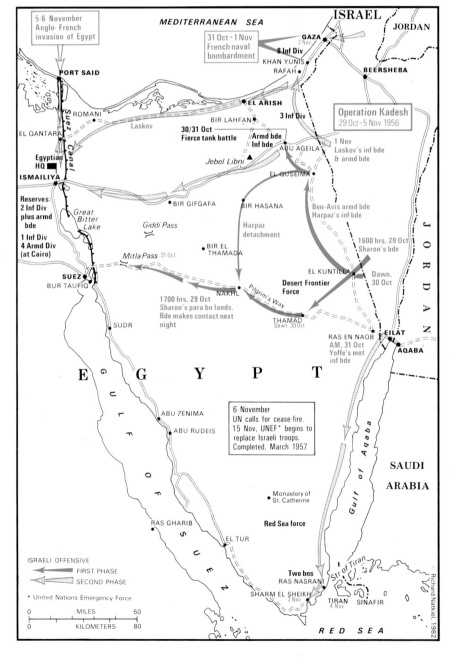

west towards the Canal pursued by Israeli tanks. Operations to subdue the remaining strongpoints in the Abu Ageila area now continued.

Back at the Mitla Pass, Arik Sharon, commander of the Israeli parachute brigade, had requested a change in the original plan, which was merely to block the eastern end in order to prevent Egyptian reinforcements being sent forward. His current position was vulnerable to Egyptian air attack and he was worried about possible counter-attacks from the Bir Gifgafa direction. Consequently, it was agreed that he could reconnoiter forward into the pass. The paratroopers became embroiled in a very bitter battle, 160 of them becoming casualties. Yet, by the time darkness fell, the pass was in Israeli hands and the Egyptian brigade there was withdrawing back to the Canal.

During the 31st another fierce battle raged,

Above: *Israeli infantry move up for the attack on Rafah which cut off the Gaza Strip.*

Left: *Mopping up El Arish after its capture on 2 November 1956.*

Below: *Egyptian artillery captured at El Ageila.*

this for Rafah. The Israelis began their attack just before midnight the previous evening. The Rafah defenses consisted of several strongpoints and extensive minefields. Intense artillery fire and Egyptian searchlights also played their part in making the break-in operation a slow one and it was not until dawn on 1 November that 27th Armored Brigade could be unleashed and sent westwards along the coast road towards the Canal. That evening its advanced guard arrived in front of El Arish, but, knowing that the Egyptians had reinforced the town with troops sent from the other side of the Canal, Dayan decided to wait until the following morning before attacking. Besides, his supply system, which was heavily reliant on civilian vehicles, had become very stretched and needed time to catch up with the advance.

The fighting in the Abu Ageila area continued throughout 1 November as one strongpoint after another was reduced. Finally, that night the Egyptians withdrew from the last of them, Um-Katef, which lay just east of Abu Ageila itself. It had held against all the Israelis could throw at it and it was only fear of being cut off which made the defenders vacate the position. With the fall of Um-Katef the heart of the Egyptian defence of Sinai had been torn out and the Israelis could now enter the exploitation phase. In the north 27th Armored Brigade entered El Arish on the morning of the 2nd and by evening its leading elements had reached Romani, just ten miles from the Canal. That they did not advance further west was because the British and French, fearful that fighting on it might damage the infrastructure of the Canal, had warned the Israelis to halt ten miles from it. Simultaneously, the Gaza Strip was cleared of opposition, which, because it had now been isolated, was negligible. In the center the Israeli forces advanced towards the other passes from Abu Ageila, while 202nd Parachute Brigade, which had remained in the Mitla Pass after its battle there on the 31st, sent a task force to Ras Sudr on the Gulf of Suez. Here it turned south towards the tip of the peninsula.

The final mission was to seize Sharm el Sheikh. The Israeli brigade tasked to do this had crossed into Sinai northwest of Eilat on 1 November. Easily brushing aside elements of the Light Mobile Frontier Force, it advanced 60 miles south on that day. Having been resupplied by sea at Dahab on the 3rd, it reached and took Sharm el Skeikh very shortly after. On the 5th, as the Anglo-French landings, airborne and amphibious, took place in the Port Said area, the captors of Sharm el Sheikh joined hands with the paratroopers who had driven down the west coast. Thus, Sinai had been totally overrun in the space of eight days. It cost the Israelis just 800 casualties. The Egyptians,

on the other hand, lost 15,000, including many taken prisoner, as well as large numbers of guns and vehicles.

As was to become the pattern with Arab-Israeli conflicts, it was the UN which brought the hostilities, both between the British and French and Egyptians, and the Israelis and Egyptians, to an end. A ceasefire was agreed on 6 November. The Anglo-French Forces were withdrawn by Christmas and the Israelis from Sinai in March 1957. In return the Egyptians guaranteed rights of passage to all shipping through the Suez Canal and to Israeli shipping in the Gulf of Aqaba, while the UN deployed peacekeeping forces at Sharm el Sheikh and in the Gaza Strip.

The Israelis had won a devastating victory in

Top: *Bemused Egyptian prisoners at Sharm el Sheikh. The speed of the Israeli advance took them totally by surprise.*

Above: *Canadian General Burns, commanding the United Nations Emergency Force (UNEF), negotiates with Moshe Dayan over the Israeli withdrawal from Sinai.*

Right: *A Norwegian tanker leaves Port Said after being trapped for two months in the blocked Suez Canal. The photograph was taken from the bullet-scarred Port Said lighthouse.*

Below: *Anglo-French commanders awaiting the arrival of UNEF commander General Burns prior to arranging the relief of their forces by UN troops. Left to right: Gen André Beaufre, Gen Sir Charles Keightley, Adm Pierre Barzot, Gen Sir Hugh Stockwell.*

Sinai, achieving all their objectives in a mere eight days. While it was a military disaster for Egypt, it was not that her troops had fought badly. Rather, it was the brilliance of the Israeli plan, combined with the determination of their troops to achieve their objectives, which had brought it about. Politically, though, Egypt did gain. International condemnation of the Anglo-French expedition won her sympathy and the fact that Nasser had stood up to the West boosted his reputation so that he was regarded as the champion of the Arab world. Thus, his defeat in Sinai became obscured by all this. Nevertheless, the desire for revenge against Israel grew among the Arabs and meant that further conflicts were inevitable. With them would come further military disasters at Israeli hands.

INDEX

Page numbers in *italics* refer to illustrations

Acknowledgments

The Publisher would like
to thank the following for
their help in the
preparation of this book:
Mike Rose the designer,
Ron Watson for the
index, Veronica Price for
production and Judith
Millidge for editing it.
We are also grateful to
the following individuals
and agencies for use of
the illustrations on the
pages noted below.
API/World Photos 1, 173
below, 174, 178-9, 183
top, 186
Africana Museum 67
(all 3), 73
Bettmann Archive
pages: 6 both, 7, 22 top,
23 top, 24 bottom pair,
26 top, 27 top and below,
29, 40-41, 47 top, 161 top,
162 top, 164 top, 165 top,
166-7, 168 below, 169
below, 170, 171 all four,
172 both, 173 top, 176
both, 189 top
**Bildarchiv Preussischer
Kulturbesitz** pages: 38
below, 39 below
Bison Picture Library
pages: 4-5, 18-19, 20 both,
21, 25, 27 middle, 28 top,
30-31, 33, 34, 35 below,
36 both, 37 both, 49
bottom pair, 52 top, 53
both, 56 below, 57 below,
59 top, 60 below, 61 top,
62-3, 63, 64, 65 both, 68,
69, 70 top, 72, 77 top, 86
below, 87 both, 93 top,
104-5 both, 106 below,
107 both, 108, 109 both,
110 top, 111 right pair, 112
all three, 113 both, 114
bottom pair, 115 left pair,
116-117, 118 below, 120
bottom, 123 bottom, 125
right pair, 126-7, 128 all
3, 131 right pair, 133
above, 136, 137 both,
138-9, 140 both, 142 both,
143, 144, 145 all 3, 146-7,
148, 149, 150 top left, 151
middle 2, 152 below, 153,
154-5, 156 both, 157 all 3,
158-9 all 3, 160, 161
below, 162 below, 163,
164 below, 168 top, 169
top, 175 all 4, 177 both,
181 top, 182 top
**Anne S K Brown
Military Collection**
pages: 50-51, 55 top
Brown University page:
58 top
Peter Clayton pages: 10,
12 both, 13 both, 16
Cliché des Musées

Nationaux, Paris page:
32 below
Peter Connolly pages: 11
both, 15 both
**Mary Evans Picture
Library** page: 32 top
**Hulton Picture
Company** pages: 8, 87
below
Robert Hunt Library
pages: 39, 52 below, 56
top, 57 top, 60 top, 61
below, 66 below, 74-75,
77 below, 79 both, 80
both, 81 below, 83 top,
84-5, 86 top, 88, 89 both,
90 both, 91, 94-5, 96 all 3,
97 top, 98 both, 99 both,
100, 101 both, 102 both,
103 all 3, 117, 119 top, 121
both, 122 both, 123 top,
124 all 3, 125 left, 129, 130
both, 132 both, 133
below, 134 middle, 135 all
3
Imperial War Museum
pages: 106 top, 110
bottom 2, 111 left pair,
114 top, 115 top right, 119
all 3, 118 middle, 120 top,
131 left, 134 top and
bottom, 141, 146, 150 (2),
151 top and bottom left,
152 top, 153 right pair,
165 below, 185 middle
**Israeli Government
Press Office** pages: 180
all 3, 181 below, 182
below, 183 bottom 2,
184-5 top 3, 187 all 3, 188
both
Library of Congress
pages: 43 both, 42
bottom 2, 44-5, 46, 47
bottom 2, 48 below, 69
top
MARS pages 14, 76
Musée de l'Armee page:
55 bottom pair
National Archives
pages: 42 top, 70 top
National Army Museum
pages: 26 below, 35 top,
66 top, 71
**National Maritime
Museum** pages: 23
below, 28 below
Novosti pages: 81 top,
82, 83 below
Ullstein pages: 82, 93
below
US Navy Museum
pages: 26 below, 35 top
**Yale University Art
Gallery** pages: 2-3